CASH
CONFIDENT

AN ENTREPRENEUR'S GUIDE TO CREATING A PROFITABLE BUSINESS

MELISSA HOUSTON

Post Hill
PRESS

A POST HILL PRESS BOOK
ISBN: 978-1-63758-636-5
ISBN (eBook): 978-1-63758-637-2

Cash Confident:
An Entrepreneur's Guide to Creating a Profitable Business
© 2023 by Melissa Houston

Cover design by Conroy Accord

Post Hill Press
New York • Nashville
posthillpress.com

Published in the United States of America
1 2 3 4 5 6 7 8 9 10

To my Dad, for believing his little girl could do anything.

TABLE OF CONTENTS

CHAPTER 1

WHAT IS CASH CONFIDENCE?

"It takes as much energy to wish as it does to plan."
— ELEANOR ROOSEVELT

Young girls and women are taught and exposed to so many limiting beliefs: be small, play small, and speak small. But we got tired of being complacent, holding ourselves back and not taking up any space, so we started challenging ourselves to show up, be heard, and above all, love ourselves. The tides are shifting: women are running organizations, many of which are represented in the C suite. Women are closing that pay gap and starting more companies than ever before. The world needs women, and the world needs us to show up in everything we do.

Fundera by nerdwallet.com reported that there are more than 12.3 million female entrepreneurs and business owners by the latest calculations,[1] and that number is growing. If you picked up this book, I'm betting you're one of them or have dreams of being one. I'm guessing you've also learned one of the most important lessons for any business owner: managing your money is *the* most important aspect of business.

The reality is that 82 percent of businesses fail due to financial mismanagement. That's why you must invest the time it takes to understand how to successfully manage the finances of your business. Learning even a few new strategies will help you optimize the profit your business generates and improve the odds of keeping your business in business for the long term. Your business is the fastest way to create wealth for yourself.

Plus, there are self-care benefits. Knowing how to manage the money in your business will alleviate those sleepless nights and reduce the tension in your stomach during the day. It will keep you healthier and more productive in your business.

Marketing, sales, social media, customer service, distribution—all these things are incredibly important. But if you're not focused on your cash flow from making a profit, none of it matters.

Becoming cash confident—knowing how to manage your money in your business and personal finances so that you are in financial control and creating wealth for yourself—is what sets you up for optimal success. Being cash confident is being willing to put yourself out there, face rejection, and recognize that a "no" simply means "not now." It means getting com-

---

1   Maddie Shepherd, "Women-Owned Businesses: Statistics and Overview (2021)," Fundera by NerdWallet, December 16, 2020, https://www.fundera.com/resources/women-owned-business-statistics.

fortable with the fact that you will always be learning and growing as an entrepreneur and making mistakes in your business regardless of what stage you are at.

My client Christine learned that the hard way. Christine reached out to me in 2020 when the COVID-19 pandemic first hit, and she knew at that moment if she didn't get help with her finances in her business then she was going to lose the successful web design agency she had spent five years building.

Christine had a great client list, many paying clients, and lots of steady revenue. But at the end of each month, she struggled to pay off the credit cards she was carrying for business debt. She wondered where it all went.

Her accountant would run her income statement for her, and she could see that she was making money, but didn't understand much more than that. She was frustrated with her relationship with her accountant as she expected him to help her more, but he didn't.

She was left feeling lost when it came to her business finances. She was embarrassed that she had let it get that bad, and she felt stupid because she had no idea how to deal with it. It was all so overwhelming that she just wanted to curl up with a sleeve of Oreos and cry.

Tears are commonplace in my office, and I believe that if you feel like crying, you should cry it out. Then get up and do something about it. That's what this book is going to help you do. Running a business isn't easy, but it's worth it.

There has never been more opportunity to create wealth for yourself than there has been in this digital age. You have the power to reach millions, if not billions, of potential clients and customers through the internet.

Cash is the lifeblood of your business, and your entire money management system will revolve around cash flow. Seeing how it all works together and knowing what you need to monitor as the CEO of your business will help you succeed—to whatever heights you desire.

You don't need to get into the weeds of accounting, but as the CEO of your business it's essential to have a high-level understanding of the finances in your business, and more importantly, how your business creates profit. Having this information will help you make better decisions in your business on a daily basis because you will know how your decisions will affect your bottom line, which is your profit.

BE THE CEO *AND* THE CFO OF YOUR BUSINESS

A chief financial officer (CFO) is the top finance person in the organization. It is their duty to help the chief executive officer (CEO) with the financial decisions. If you're a small or growing business, chances are you haven't hired a full-time CFO yet, but even if you did, it's your business and you need to understand the financial information of your own business. It makes you a better business owner and CEO.

You don't need to stop working with your bookkeeper or your accountant, but you do need to be involved and understand your business numbers.

Have you heard stories about celebrities losing millions of dollars because of bad managers? They always follow a similar formula: a greedy money manager who assumes no one will notice them siphoning off money and spending frivolously without any checks and balances. It is believed that most people wouldn't normally steal, but when the right opportunity presents itself, they will. It's too tempting when the opportunity presents itself and they know they probably won't get caught. And this isn't just happening to the rich and famous. The best way you can protect yourself is to be involved in the finances of your business. Nobody will ever care about your business as much as you do, so never give your financial power away.

You need to protect your money and your wealth and not blindly trust others to make the best decisions for you and your business.

You are in control. When you know your numbers and are involved in your finances, you won't be giving your financial power away. You can seek expert opinions, and then you will clearly understand the nature of the advice being offered. But you will also have the ability to take their opinion into consideration and come up with a solution that is best for your business. Because you know your business the best, you're better positioned to make those financial decisions.

When clients come to see me, they are usually feeling overwhelmed by the state of their business finances. They'd prefer to avoid looking at their business performance altogether for fear of what they may find. Clients often tell me that they're no good with numbers or that it will take them way longer to learn how to manage their finances than the average person.

Tina, a podcast producer, was a perfect example of this. She felt that she was going to be a unique case and someone who wouldn't learn easily due to her ADHD. But as we walked through the eight-week program together, taking it step by step, her fear of looking at her numbers dissipated and her confidence grew.

We worked through the five-step Cash Confident Framework™ together over the eight-week program, and she absorbed each step of the framework with ease. Because the steps were broken down into manageable pieces and included real-life examples that applied to her business, and because the information was relatable, it was far easier for Tina to absorb it.

We created her business financial plan, where we not only looked at where she was in her business but took into account the goals that she wanted to achieve over the next twelve months. She wanted to create a six-figure business with profit margins of 30 percent. We worked through that plan and built it out over the year.

She started piecing together how the way she managed her business finances was reflected in the way she managed her business as a whole, and she didn't like it. She knew that to be the best business owner she could be, she would have to step up her business game and step into the role of a business owner who understood how to manage their finances.

What really resonated with Tina was creating that business plan so she could plan a year ahead and clearly understand the moving parts that she would need to achieve in order to reach her goals. With the business financial plan came clarity for her business and what she wanted to achieve for the year ahead.

Having that financial plan gave Tina the confidence she needed to pursue her financial goals.

Fast forward to two years later and Tina is still planning her business finances, she has a secure financial plan in place, she has increased her profit margins through increased revenue, she has made her business more efficient, and she now works less in her business as she enjoys more money for herself.

Tina makes regular money dates with her business, reviews her personal and business financial goals regularly, and makes sure she keeps herself accountable to these goals through planning and monitoring her progress.

Tina has plans to buy a house soon and start a family. She's excited about her future and no longer stresses about it because she has a plan and she knows that planning out her finances works.

THE FIRST STEP: YOU MUST THINK LIKE A CFO

I realize this step sounds scary, but please remember that I'm not asking you to actually be a CFO, just think more like one. A CFO thinks strategically and wants the business to make as much profit as possible.

Money makes us emotional. Money is a tool we use to purchase our needs and wants, yet it creates so much emotion. It measures our self-worth and feelings of adequacy. It fuels our desires, and if we mismanage our money, it leads us to shame and embarrassment.

Our credit scores, debt levels, and net worth are all measured by how we manage our money.

Money can drive us crazy.

Money is the most emotionally charged topic there is. And that's why when you learn to think like a CFO, there's no room for attaching emotion to money.

In business, money is the numbers. The business numbers are feedback, and they tell you how your business is performing. They're not there to judge you; they're there to help you.

Your business will always be changing and evolving as it grows, and the numbers are there to steer you in the right direction. They offer insight, advice, and guidance into growing and scaling your business. They are honest. Numbers don't lie.

That's why as the CEO of your business it's important to take the emotion out of the money.

Did you know that your business has the potential to be your largest financial asset? Did you know that if you allow yourself to dream big and set lofty financial goals for yourself that chances are you can achieve them through your business?

Every activity in your business affects your bottom line, whether that is directly or indirectly. There is nothing that happens in business that doesn't translate to either improving or depleting the bottom line of your business. That bottom line is also known as your profit line, and profit is the most important aspect of your business.

There are many moving parts in the financial management of your business, but if you are not making a profit—which is revenue less expenses—then your business will fail.

Profit is the money that you get to keep for yourself at the end of the day. It's what makes your wallet fat and increases your net worth. Profit makes you wealthy. This book is going to help you achieve that wealth so that you can live the financial life of your dreams.

Financial leadership is important for any CEO or business owner to possess. Successful businesswomen know their financial numbers and the financial health of their businesses. Why? Because when you know your business numbers you understand how your business operates. When you know your business numbers, you understand your business on an intimate level.

I'm not talking about getting lost in the weeds of your business. What I believe every CEO of their business needs to understand is the high-level financial information that will help you make profitable decisions. You don't need to know how to calculate the net present value of a project that a trained CPA would know. But you do need to know what's going on to make profitable business decisions.

So why would you want to learn how to manage your finances? Why do you need to think like a CFO, and what's in it for you?

Good questions.

Are you a traditional business owner? Do you want to make money in your business and grow your business? Do you want to be a rich business owner? Do you want to be the CEO of your business and not be taken advantage of by others?

If you said yes to any of those questions, then that's why you need to manage your business finances as well. Nobody will mess with you if you know your business numbers.

You will have unshakeable confidence when you know your business numbers because financial empowerment is significant, especially to women. It allows you to step into the role of powerhouse. You will have the information that you need to make confident and profitable business decisions.

Yes, you could have an accountant or business manager handle your money for you. But why would you? That would be giving your financial power away. There are far too many stories of wealthy people who have trusted others to manage their money for them, only to find out that they've lost millions, and in some cases everything, to shady business money managers. When you get involved in your business finances this prevents these things from happening.

I'm not suggesting replacing your accountant; rather, I'm encouraging you to get involved. You don't need to get in the weeds of GAAP and tax returns, but you do need to oversee and have an understanding of how your finances affect your business. When you understand how your business creates profit that enables you to make more profitable decisions on a daily basis.

You can still use the advice of others, but don't check out of your business finances (or personal finances for that matter). Be involved, know your money, and don't ever give your financial power away.

When you invest the time into understanding at a high level how to run your business finances, you are learning a new business skill that will provide value and increase profitability many times over for years to come. Essentially this means that you will be making more money for yourself. It will keep more money in your pocket and increase your net worth.

Leadership is not only about making tough decisions like layoffs and cost-cutting but also about leading an organization through the financial side of the business. You need to speak about profit margins, income statements, budgets, and financial concerns. When we normalize women in leadership positions and their ability to manage their company's money, you can speak to your team about money management in the business.

Making space for money talks and wealth management is an important and essential aspect of money management.

We need to normalize women making money, and lots of it.

The best way to make money is through your business. And the best way to hold onto that money and grow your wealth is through excellent money management skills.

The wealthiest people in the world know these secrets, and I want you to know them too.

There is no room in our society for anything less than equality, and we need to narrow the gender pay gap as well.

According to Fidelity's 2021 Women and Investing study, when it comes to investing, women outperform men by forty basis points on average. This positive margin can translate to thousands of dollars over time, depending on the amount invested.

CNBC reported that in addition, women have been making significant gains in accumulating assets, with 67 percent of female investors surveyed saving beyond their retirement accounts, up from 44 percent in 2018. Meanwhile, nearly 50 percent have saved $20,000 or more outside their retirement accounts and emergency funds, with 20 percent saving

$100,000 or more. These extra savings can mean considerable assets over the long term.

You need to use your business skills and financial skills to build your empire. You deserve your business empire just as much as Elon Musk, Bill Gates, and all the other men who are dominating the wealth in the world.

But there are also women who dominate world wealth. In Forbes's 2021 list of the world's billionaires, 328 women were featured, which was an increase of 36 percent from the year before. The list included names such as Alice Walton, MacKenzie Scott, Yang Huiyan, and Whitney Wolfe Herd.

Transform yourself into the powerful leader that I know you are. Develop the unshakable confidence that I know you can have and get those skills sharpened to help you step into that new leadership role. Be the woman who goes after her goals and knows that what she has to offer the world is just as valuable, if not more, than the Musks and Gateses of the world.

By getting comfortable with financial speak you will promote your leadership position and elevate your authority. Accounting is the language of business, and by being well-versed against colleagues and competitors in financial speak, you are elevating your role as a business owner. You will be informed and educated and at a level with others in the room when talking about profit and loss statements and financial metrics.

You see, the numbers in your business are telling you a story. And the harsh reality is that numbers don't lie. If your business is floundering, you will know, and your numbers will tell you exactly where you are lacking, and that is useful feed-back to correct it when you are in a financial routine. You will look at reports regularly and catch minor issues before they become big problems and money drains.

This allows you to lead fearlessly, to be a boss who makes profitable decisions, clear and decisive decisions, and to be a leader who a team can rally behind.

Who am I to guide you on this journey?

My name is Melissa Houston, and I'm a Chartered Professional Accountant (CPA) with over twenty years of busi-ness experience. I can get you excited about making money and making lots of it. I help business owners get behind their businesses as the leader they are meant to be with unshak-able confidence and determination. I am the founder of She Means Profit™, which is a blog and podcast aimed at helping business owners like you optimize profit in your business so that you can keep more money in your pocket and increase your net worth.

Throughout my career, I have worked with various types of business owners and stakeholders who don't understand the value of understanding their business numbers, and I have helped transform them into top leaders in their industry, because what I teach matters. Money matters.

I will teach you and support you in getting the wealth that you've dreamed of and that you deserve. I will teach you that the secret to success in business is knowing your business numbers. And I will teach you the financial language that you need to know to be on the same page as your accountant, your banker, your VCFO, and your business colleagues.

I will help you achieve this by offering you step-by-step advice and guidance and showing you my signature five-step Cash Confident Framework™ that has helped countless business owners gain financial control of their businesses, and you can too!

These steps include:

Step 1: Master your money mindset.

This is where it all begins. Money is the most emotionally charged topic out there, and everyone carries money baggage, sometimes from their earliest childhood memories. Everyone has an opinion about money, rich people, and poor people.

Step 2: Know your financial reports.

Reading and understanding your financial reports is a vital part of being a business owner. Financial reports are a way of communicating how the business is doing and giving you feedback on where you can improve performance and optimize profitability.

Step 3: Create a financial plan.

A business financial plan is a smart way to put your business goals into an actionable plan. It offers a roadmap for your business and helps you understand what you need to do in order to achieve your business goals.

Step 4: Monitor your progress.

Once you have that financial plan in place it is essential to monitor your progress against that plan at a minimum of once every month. It is through monitoring that you can make adjustments to reach your goals by year-end.

Step 5: Manage your cash flow.

Cash is the lifeline of your business. Think of it as the blood coursing through your body. Without it you would be dead. Your business needs cash flowing in and out in an organized manner to protect its survival. Be sure you have a cash management system in place.

The bottom line is when you get comfortable with the financial reports in your business and understand the financial talk, you will benefit from that effort and your business will be more profitable.

Sara is a successful business owner who partnered with another female co-founder and shared her adventures in building her business. They are truly taking the business world by storm, but it almost didn't turn out that way.

Sara told me her money story. When she and her partner had received funding and had a large sum of money in the bank, Sara's partner was granted the task of dealing with all the financials of the business even though the business belonged to both of them.

As cash outlays are huge when starting a business, the business's bank account was dwindling. Sara was none the wiser because she had happily checked out of the business finances and left the responsibility completely up to her partner.

When her partner informed her of the impending cash flow issue, Sara confessed that she felt angry and resented her

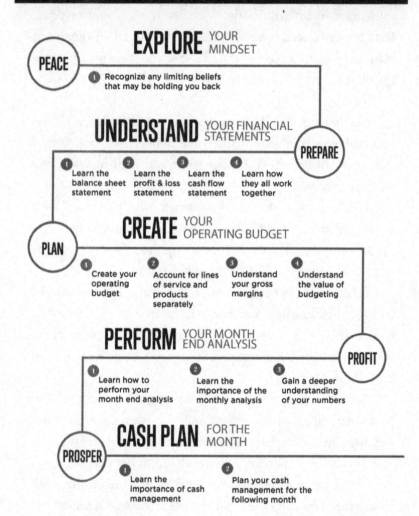

the CASH CONFIDENT
FRAMEWORK™

PEACE

EXPLORE YOUR MINDSET

1 Recognize any limiting beliefs that may be holding you back

UNDERSTAND YOUR FINANCIAL STATEMENTS

PREPARE

1 Learn the balance sheet statement

2 Learn the profit & loss statement

3 Learn the cash flow statement

4 Learn how they all work together

CREATE YOUR OPERATING BUDGET

PLAN

1 Create your operating budget

2 Account for lines of service and products separately

3 Understand your gross margins

4 Understand the value of budgeting

PERFORM YOUR MONTH END ANALYSIS

PROFIT

1 Learn how to perform your month end analysis

2 Learn the importance of the monthly analysis

3 Gain a deeper understanding of your numbers

CASH PLAN FOR THE MONTH

PROSPER

1 Learn the importance of cash management

2 Plan your cash management for the following month

partner for not taking care of things. This money rift could have killed the partnership. But thankfully the partners pulled through via more fundraising.

However, this was not a lesson lost on Sara. After much reflection and looking at the situation without emotion, Sara came to realize that this was just as much her doing as it was her partner's. Sara realized how completely unfair it was to be inaccessible when it came time to talk about finances and to expect her partner to deal with it all.

Now Sara is showing up as an equal partner in the business. The partners have established regular money meetings where they discuss the finances of the business, its financial health, where the business is heading in terms of meeting financial goals, and the state of the cash flow forecasting.

You see, Sara had not been acting as the CEO of her business when it came to understanding and being involved in the business finances. A large part of being an effective CEO of your business is to know and understand your business finances. You need a high-level understanding of what is going on with your business numbers. You need to read your monthly financial statements, understand the profitability of your business and how it is generated, and measure your performance against your goals.

When you know your business numbers you know your business intimately. You don't need to be an accountant to think like a CFO; you just need to understand the high-level financial information so that you can align the vision of the business with the actual path to get there.

Years later, Sara's company is a growing and thriving business, and the partnership remains solid as both partners are equally invested in the financial health of the business and the business as a whole.

KEY TAKEAWAYS:

1. Women have what it takes to run successful, profitable businesses—don't ever doubt that. We need to normalize women building wealth for themselves. Women are good with money, and I know you can do this!
2. Be the CEO and the CFO of your business. When you think like a chief financial officer, it helps you create the profitability in your business to create wealth for yourself.
3. Don't give up your financial power. You don't need to be an accountant in your business, but you do need to have smart conversations with your accountant! Surround yourself with people who will encourage you and lift you up, as you will do with them.
4. Your business might be the largest financial asset you will own if you create profit and manage the money well. Create wealth through your business and become rich!

CHAPTER 2

STEP 1: MASTER YOUR MONEY MINDSET

"Money, like emotions, is something you must control to keep your life on the right track."
— Natasha Munson

Thoughts alone have no real power, but when you engage with them or give them attention, they begin to influence your reality. If you believe you're not good with money, you may immediately start to feel defensive or discouraged when you're reading a financial report or asked about your profits. But if you flip that thought around and tell yourself that you're good at managing money, then you'll start to think more positive thoughts and boost your confidence.

In my opinion, thinking positively about your money skills is the most important step—you need to believe that you are worthy of money. The Pareto Principle suggests that money management is 20 percent knowledge and 80 percent behavior, so your mindset deserves attention while negative thoughts, patterns, and relationships need to be corrected to create wealth.

Part of the challenge is that many of us don't even recognize sneaky limiting beliefs because they are deep in our subconscious. We think we control our thoughts, but a study published in the journal *Scientific Reports* shows that your brain initiates a command some eleven seconds ahead of you consciously having that thought.[1] If that's the case, most of the time, your brain patterns are making the decisions of how you react to a situation, which prevents you from being in the moment and dealing with what's in front of you.

Often, we doubt ourselves and our abilities and feel like frauds. This is known as imposter syndrome, which highlights our insecurities with our skillset. We carry these limiting beliefs on the subconscious level, and they're classic fodder for CEO imposter syndrome. Common ones include:

> *"I'm not innovative enough."*
> *"I'm not smart enough."*
> *"I'm not an expert in…"*
> *"I don't have enough experience…"*
> *"No one thinks I can do this."*

Now add the emotionally charged layer of money on top and it becomes a huge obstacle for business owners. If talking about money makes you mildly uncomfortable or stressed in

---

1   Koenig-Robert, R., Pearson, J. "Decoding the contents and strength of imagery before volitional engagement." *Sci Rep* 9, 3504 (2019). https://doi.org/10.1038/s41598-019-39813-y.

any way, that's a clue you have a money mindset issue. Do any of these limiting beliefs strike a chord with you?

"I'm not smart enough to manage my money well."
"It's greedy to want more money."
"I'm not good at math."
"I can just buy that on credit (ignoring the cost of carrying that balance)."
"I can always repay my debt."
"I'll never get clients to pay me for my services."
"I'll never get out of debt."
"Women aren't supposed to be rich."

Where do these thoughts come from? So much of how we think and feel about money is formed in early childhood, resulting in our adult attitudes, thoughts, and instinctual behaviors with money. It's through small interactions early in life that we learn our biggest lessons in life. Was money always in abundance in your childhood, or was it scarce? Did your parents fight about money, leaving you with anxious memories about it? Did money make you feel safe or did a lack thereof make you feel unsafe? Did anyone ever break your trust or did a relationship come under strain due to money?

Everyone has a money story. We all have money quirks and habits informed by our earliest memories, which have led to your unique relationship with managing your finances. Maybe that has turned you into a spender or a saver, or you're in debt, or money is a constant source of stress.

It's essential for everyone—and business owners in particular—to become aware of what drives their money habits, take a crash course in financial management (this book!), and learn how to make their money work harder for them.

GET TO KNOW YOUR MONEY STORY

Your money story was likely formed during your childhood. Think back to the thoughts, beliefs, and habits that your family had around money. How did your parents and grandparents relate to money? Was money scarce or abundant?

Look at who you are now. Is there conflict?

Most likely, your money story was set when you were a child based on what your parents, family, and society taught you. When you bring that money story into your adult life, it doesn't serve you.

Get clear on what your beliefs are around money so you can start to transform the negative ones and begin attracting money instead of repelling it!

Whatever the memory or feeling is, you may act in certain ways or hold an unconscious belief because of that memory. Money comes with baggage, and this can influence your mindset and habits, often without even being aware of it.

When I was nine years old, I went shopping with my mom and saw a beautiful brooch that I desperately wanted. I knew I had enough money to pay for it, but that cash was nestled in my brown wallet in the top drawer of my dresser. My mom agreed to buy it for me if I paid her back when we got home. "Deal," I said, elated. When we returned home, I ran upstairs to grab my wallet, but when I took it out, it was empty. My heart sank. I knew either my brother or sister had stolen my money from me, and I didn't know what to do. Neither of them admitted to it.

My mom showed little sympathy for me and made me pay back that money, cent by cent. It took me a few weeks of allowance to do so, but once I did, I felt great. I know my mom wanted to teach me a lesson about money and responsibility, but sadly the only lesson I took away was that it was easy to buy things on credit.

Through the years, my mother unknowingly supported my credit habit. When I was eighteen, I wanted to buy a car. My parents lent me the money and I paid them back. When I went to college, I got my first credit card. I also got a line of credit from the bank. The only thing I understood about those two things was that whatever I borrowed had to be paid back. I was responsible. I made my payments on time and paid it off. Easy enough! I was clueless about my interest rate or how much money I was throwing away.

My parents had good intentions and I have always appreciated their financial advice and support, but what I learned at a young age was to be comfortable with debt. It never bothered me to have a credit card balance or know I owed someone money. I knew I would pay it off eventually. It took a while for me to understand that when I carried debt with credit cards and lines of credit, the high interest was killing my bottom line. Also, having some credit card debt was damaging to my psyche, my savings, and my health.

IDENTIFY YOUR MONEY BLOCKS

What's your money story? How would you describe your relationship with money? And what is holding you back from building your most profitable business?

When I first meet with new clients, I try to get to know them as people—not learn more about their business right away. I want to understand their money mindset and the teachings, experiences, and lessons they've internalized that may have led to limiting beliefs. I try to get them to open up, reflect, and talk to me about their money story.

Your money story can stem from your childhood or more recent successes and challenges. If you were raised in a home where money was a stressor, debt was always present, and there was never enough money to pay bills, those emotions will affect how you view debt to keep your business in scarcity mode.

Or maybe your parents never talked about money and always told you "not to worry about it," so you didn't. And now you avoid money conversations and never look at your business's financial reports. Or maybe your money story is a new one: you have your own family to support, and you want a financially secure future that means millions of dollars in assets, but you are too afraid to fail.

My clients and I do an exercise where we walk down our money memory lane and think about moments along the way. You can do this, too—ask yourself:

- How did your parents handle money?
- Was money talked about at home?

- Were your parents always worried about money?
- What were your early memories of money?
- How did you feel when you got your first job?
- What did that feel like to have your own money?
- When you hear the word *money*, do you feel good about it?
- Do you feel fearful about it? Why?

Tune in to your thoughts and emotions. Ask yourself why. Once you identify your limiting beliefs, you can start to address them and take their power away. When I start connecting the dots with my clients' money stories and their current money habits, it's a real "aha" moment. I have clients tell me, "Oh my gosh, I'm handling money this way because this is what I saw at home."

My client Susan was eight years old when her mom sent her to the store to buy some milk (yes, we were allowed to do that in the eighties!). Susan put that money in her pocket to keep it safe. On her way to the store, she met up with friends who were playing hopscotch. Susan stopped to play with them for a bit then went on her way, and when Susan got to the store, she realized that the money for the milk must have fallen out of her pocket. She was scared to tell her mom what had happened but knew she had to. Susan's mom scolded her, told her that she was no good with money, and sent her to her room as punishment. Ever since that event, Susan told herself that she was not good with money.

As an adult, Susan always spent money right away and never saved it. She kept telling herself she was simply no good with it. I'm not trying to lay blame on parental mistakes; this is about dealing with the cards you've been dealt and recovering from them. But all that changed when I helped Susan identify her internal beliefs around money and reset those beliefs.

Together, we explored how she felt about money. Susan allowed herself to search back in her memory to a time when she felt like a failure with money. This story surfaced and she felt the pain all over again, just like it had happened that day.

But Susan learned how to identify that pain and feel it. She breathed through it, and when she was ready to release it, she let that pain go. The trouble with childhood pain is that we aren't equipped to deal with it and we hang on tightly to it. It follows us into adulthood, and we don't even realize it's there. But it weighs us down.

With that release, Susan was able to start living in the present and reset her beliefs. One way she did that was to find quotes that inspired her and reminded her that she could let go of the past and step into the person she is today. So, when Susan caught herself thinking about how she was no good with money, she reprogrammed that thought process with the quotes. She put reminders everywhere in her environment—bathroom mirror, computer screen, in her phone. She took a minute to absorb that. When she became triggered to think she was no good with money, she replaced those thoughts with the reminder that yes, she is.

FLIP THE SWITCH AND REFRAME YOUR MONEY STORY

Think about how you are making financial decisions. Does it come from fear? Does that fear hold you back from receiving money?

When I realized that my relationship with money was negative, you best believe I did the work to flip the switch. I am now very clear on my goals of creating wealth for myself and my family, and I was determined not to shortchange us.

So how do we create new, helpful thought habits about money? Like any habit, the first step is to create a routine. To evaluate your thoughts throughout the day, ask yourself these simple questions:

- What am I thinking about money right now? What am I feeling?
- Is this thought/feeling helping me reach my desired financial outcome?

If the answer is "no" to either, redirect your thoughts and beliefs. It's with practice that this will come more naturally. Make your dreams nonnegotiable. Mindset needs to be checked in regularly—it's not a "set it and forget it" solution.

Trust your gut instincts and follow your heart, and believe you are meant for more. This isn't just about money; it's about the opportunities that are available to you in life as well. When you have a growth mindset you believe that anything is possible, even with money.

For example, when I set out to write this book, the amount of negativity that came to me was overwhelming. People argued that since I was a first-time author, I'd never get a deal. They said my audience was too small, everyone wants to write a book, nobody wants to read about money, and the list goes on.

Yet, I knew in my gut that this was what I wanted to do. I persevered, and here we are. And you are reading this book!

When you believe in yourself, anything is possible.

Let go of what people think about you. This is the true key to happiness. You don't need everyone to like you. I often tell people that what other people think of you is none of your business. Let that go because you are not here to make them happy. It's part of protecting your energy and preventing others' thoughts, moods, and actions from affecting you.

CHALLENGE YOUR BELIEFS

Limiting beliefs, attitudes, and behaviors are compounded by persistent societal myths about women and money: Women don't have the head for business! Boys are better at math! Women are too emotional to understand finance!

One poll found that boys were more likely than girls to learn about investing, taxes, and credit scores from their parents. It's not surprising, then, that men report having more financial confidence than women and that UBS Global Wealth found that 56 percent of women leave investment decisions to their husbands.[2] These negative mixed messages are then repeated in the media. Anne Boden, founder and CEO of

---

2   UBS Media, "UBS reveals top reason married women step aside in long-term financial decisions: They believe their husbands know more," May 14, 2018, https://www.ubs.com/global/de/media/display-page-ndp/en-20180514-ubs-reveals-top-reason.html.

Starling Bank, commissioned a study that found about 65 percent of financial articles in women's magazines categorized women as excessive spenders while 70 percent of the ones aimed at men emphasized making money.[3] These messages create a damaging pattern where women find themselves with a lack of financial literacy and fear of money.

I've had clients deny that they have money mindset issues. When I worked with Gina, I asked how she felt about sales, and she was quick to respond that she loved sales and she was a killer at it, and she went so far as to say it was her strongest skill as an entrepreneur. But as we continued to work together, it became clear that Gina had a major sales issue. She *was* amazing at sales for other people and products, but she really struggled with owning her own value and setting prices for her products and services. I see this all the time. Women often undercharge because of persistent messages that they're not good enough to charge a high rate or that people will laugh at them. Being in your own business makes you vulnerable and exposed. You need to be in a good headspace to not fall victim to this.

I talked to Gina about the importance of breaking the bonds between emotions and money. Pricing is nothing to take personally. If someone does scoff at what you're offering, move on, because they don't value you and you don't want to work with them anyway. Use it to your advantage to pave the way. What I tell clients is to detach from the negative emotions of money and instead flip them on their head. One way

---

3   Kristin Wong, "The Myth of the Frivolous Female Spender," *The New York Times*, October 4, 2019, https://www.nytimes.com/2019/10/04/us/myth-frivolous-female-spender.html

to do this is to define your core values and what is important to you. Many of my clients list health, family, safety, and security as core values. The essential next step is exploring why and how they relate to their finances. Then they can create goals around those specific values. For example, if family is a core value, your personal finance goals may be saving for your children's education, taking family vacations together, or living within your means to create a stress-free household. This leads to financial values and a foundation for making smarter money decisions.

The same is true with your business. What are your broader business values? If creating a legacy company is one of your values, you'll want to develop financial goals that set up your company for steady long-term growth and profit. If giving back to the community is an important value, you will need enough cushion in your budget to fund philanthropy and thus must make some conservative spending choices.

Think about the last time you were deciding whether or not to make an investment in your business. Maybe the cost of a virtual assistant seemed expensive at the time, and you decided not to go for it, and instead gave your graphic designer a raise because you deemed her work and her time essential. Your priority was to keep your graphic designer happy because her work impacts your bottom line. Your priority could just as easily have been to hire a virtual assistant to free up your own time, but your core values of employee satisfaction took priority.

When you have that North Star—that financial vision—it strengthens your money mindset. Being in control of your money and financial decisions gives you confidence, and confidence leads to power.

I know firsthand how money stories affect your business. I struggled with my own money mindset issues when I first started my business. Having been a social worker in my first career, I have always wanted to help people fix their problems. As an accountant working in firms and large businesses, I never had to expose myself to selling.

When I started my business, I had big financial goals and if anyone had asked me if I had money mindset issues, I honestly would have laughed at that thought.

But months started to go by and what I noticed was that there was something off with my sales strategy. Then I quickly learned that I had a lot of resistance around sales. I did some mindset work with my coach immediately. I found that I was holding on to money stories of my own.

I grew up upper-middle class in Canada and never went without anything. However, my family was always very mindful of their spending and were extremely hypersensitive to being "sold to." My parents did not like salespeople, and if they made a purchase, it was never under the influence of any salesperson.

I carried these beliefs with me myself and really resented those who tried selling to me, so naturally I projected my own sales beliefs onto potential clients. This did not help my sales initiative. I failed to understand that I was not "selling" them a solution, but I was offering a solution to a problem they needed fixed and inviting them to work with me if they wanted to fix that problem.

What really surprised me is that even though cognitively I knew that, and I would have told any other woman to charge what they were worth and sell with confidence, for whatever reason it didn't feel like that applied to me.

Realizing this shortcoming, I worked with a money mindset coach to resolve this issue. It took a lot of personal work around sales and seeing how I was helping people in exchange for being paid for my time and services. Building a profitable business was important to me, so I had to take the time to work out those issues and bring in money.

The effort worked really well for me and now I am very comfortable offering my services in exchange for money. I hold no attachment to the outcome and realize that sales is just another part of running a business and being an entrepreneur.

But can you imagine what would have happened to my business if I had not addressed that immediately? I would have constantly struggled with cash flow because I needed sales coming in to pay my business expenses and pay myself. I would be miserable and struggling, and the lack of sales would have kept me far away from my wealth goals.

I have financial goals of my own. Big, lofty financial goals. I feel no shame about it either because I know I can do a lot of good with that money. I also have a financial strategy that will help me reach my financial goals. Because I have that plan, I know that my dreams are possible, and I know how to get there.

KNOW YOUR WORTH

We will often talk ourselves out of something for fear that we can't do it, or we'll tell ourselves that we aren't smart enough. This is negative self-talk, and it isn't the only contributor to thwarting your profit and wealth potential. When you ignore your finances or stay complacent in the present, your money mindset suffers. I challenge clients to think of what they want out of life. Think about what you really desire. If money weren't an issue, where would you be living? What would you be doing?

Since we know that money management is primarily attributed to behavior, you really need to focus on your behavior, which is your money mindset when it comes to managing your business and personal finances. Limiting beliefs can be so ingrained in us and hold us back in various ways. As business owners, you are in a unique position to build your wealth through your business. You can grow your business to create the lifestyle that you want to support. I encourage you to do so.

But money mindset issues don't end here. You can have a real fear of making money, becoming wealthy, and the like. I feel so passionate about nurturing your money mindset and your relationship with money because if you don't, and you continue to carry around negative beliefs, you will be holding yourself back from being the best (and most profitable) business owner that you can be.

If you have done any mindset work, you likely have faced the dilemma of the scarcity mindset versus the abundance mindset. A scarcity mindset means that you fear that there will never be enough. An abundance mindset means you know that there will not only be enough for you, but for all.

As a business owner it's important to be in the abundance mindset. When you are living in abundance, you know that growth—both personal and professional—is essential in business.

Business owners and entrepreneurs make themselves vulnerable by offering their products and services to the world. You open yourselves up to criticism, ridicule, and rejection. It's not easy being an entrepreneur or business owner, and you need to keep that mindset positive or you risk losing a lot in your business. A positive mindset will help keep you going, even on the hardest of days.

Research from Consulting Success found that consultants who consciously work on their mindset make more money.[4] Out of the consultants who make over $150,000, 78 percent of them consistently work on their mindset. When I start working with clients, I first try to figure out their preconceived attitudes toward money, whether conscious or unconscious. I can give you the financial tools and resources you need to succeed, but if there's something holding you back, all the smarts in the world won't fill that hole. Your money story is part of who you are, and resetting internal beliefs takes self-awareness. Let's get started.

---

4   Michael Zipursky, "Entrepreneurial Mindset Study 2020: The Mindset of Successful Consultants," Consulting Success, https://www.consultingsuccess.com/entrepreneurial-mindset-study.

CREATE YOUR FINANCIAL GOALS

Eighty-three percent of people that set financial goals feel better about their finances after just one year, a study from Lincoln Financial Group reports. Many women entrepreneurs feel that they should be making just enough to pay their bills, but my challenge to you is, why wouldn't you want more? Do you want to drive a luxurious car, pay for your children's education, live in an upscale neighborhood, or maybe even start a nonprofit or charity? Think about those desires and think about why you aren't aiming high and dreaming big.

I have seen many women held back because they have been taught that wanting more is greedy and that it's bad to want more. I'd argue that this is not greedy. However, most women will want to earn only what they need to cover their expenses. When has making more money been a bad thing for women? Or anyone?

A lot of good can be done with money. If you have ever considered philanthropic work, making extra money in your business can allow you to increase the amount you donate to charities. You could also use that money to start your own nonprofit organization. You are in charge of your finances, and that allows you the opportunity to fulfill your financial dreams as well.

A big part of the work that I do with women entrepreneurs is challenging them to create big financial goals. As a business owner, you are in a unique position to build your wealth through your business. But the key is to want to build that wealth. Creating dreams and big financial goals can be exciting.

Yet when women are asked to create goals, a lot of old money stories come bubbling to the surface.

"Rich people are not nice people."

"I only need to make what I need."

"Being rich isn't for me."

ASSESS YOUR FINANCIAL GOALS

So often we are afraid of dreaming big for fear of failure. We shortchange ourselves because we question our worth to others. We are afraid to charge premium rates for our services, we are afraid to create wealth for ourselves, and generally we are comfortable holding ourselves back from our true goals. But anything is possible. All of your dreams can become your reality, but it starts with knowing what they are.

Ask yourself, "How much money do I want to be making in my business?" and set that intention.

By setting intentions you are committing to the results you want in your life and business. You decide how much money you want to make through your business.

What is your main goal or desired outcome for your business? Be honest and specific, and most importantly, don't shortchange yourself.

ASSESS YOUR RELATIONSHIP WITH MONEY

Know that you are worthy of your money desires. How you interact with and treat your money is a relationship. You need a positive relationship with money so that you will reach the financial rewards that you seek in life.

Ask yourself this question: What do you need to overcome in your relationship with money?

TAKE CONSISTENT ACTION

Tanya came to me with an attitude that she was never going to achieve any financial success because she didn't know what she was doing. She was having self-doubts that she was smart enough to run a profitable business. I told her, "It's not your fault! Were you ever taught basic accounting? How are you expected to know this if you've never done it before?"

"Oh, that's a good point!" she said.

The simple act of validating her worth made all the difference in the world. But the real transformation comes when people start getting into the numbers.

Tanya had tremendous fear around financial methods and language, but once I taught her the basics for entrepreneurs in manageable chunks, her confidence exploded. She realized she could do this! It was education plus action. You can talk about accounting tricks until you're blue in the face, but until you start taking control of your finances, it won't change anything.

When you start to understand that money is a tool and that it doesn't measure your success or failure, and you learn how to use that tool, I promise you, business will boom.

Sometimes you will use the tool wrongly, but know this: *your money mistakes don't define you.* It serves you no purpose to beat yourself up or deny the fact that you're not as aware of your financials as you'd like to be. Mistakes are feedback telling you that the approach you tried didn't work. I've made mistakes of every shape and size, and so has every entrepreneur. But what we all know is each one offers a lesson. Accept that there's work to be done but know that it can be done.

There is so much value in reflecting on what went wrong and how it went wrong. There are lessons in every mistake or disappointment. And these all serve to make you stronger. Lean into them. The thing one learns about business is that nothing is personal. A client used your services and never paid you for them. You accumulated too much debt. These mistakes don't define you, but they do offer you terrific lessons you can learn from. And when you come out on the other side, you will feel free. Sometimes it's hard not to take mistakes personally or as a sign it's time to quit, but if you are smart enough to take the lesson in every mistake, you will end up with a fantastic business.

Accepting a money mistake was key for money expert and author Amber Lilyestrom. Two years ago, Amber found herself facing an exorbitant tax bill. "I thought I was doing everything right, and then I felt like a failure. I felt embarrassed, ashamed, stressed out," she says. "Then I realized that in my childhood home there were always urgent letters from the IRS, which caused a lot of messaging around taxes being scary and stressful. I always would feel terrified going into those meetings with my accountant. But then I decided to take the driver's seat, and say, 'No, this isn't happening to me.' And it's just math at the end of the day, and after that I'm never going to let my accountant make me feel like that again."

If you picked up this book, I know you are a high achiever who wants to do a good job and build a successful business. If there is one thing you take from this book, it's this: money has nothing to do with your worth or how successful you are. I know that can feel counterintuitive, but to achieve real growth it's time to stop using money as the metric of success and see money as a tool to achieve that success.

Money is a tool. Remember that. That's why it's so essential you learn how to use it.

BE PREPARED TO MAKE MORE MONEY MISTAKES IN BUSINESS

Your business will always be evolving and growing. Knowing that you will be making mistakes along the way will help with maintaining a positive mindset. Mistakes happen, especially in business, and adjusting and learning from those mistakes is a valuable lesson.

The expression "fail forward" is a common one in the entrepreneurial space, and I encourage you to embrace it now to alleviate any future grief.

It will never be perfect, and as your business continues to expand and grow you will make more mistakes. But when you understand the financial consequences of certain mistakes you can make your losses smaller.

Business is about constantly evolving and changing, and you take risks and if you've planned well, rewards go with those risks.

KEY TAKEAWAYS

1. Think about your earliest lessons about money. How did your parents talk about money? What were your first experiences? Identify how your financial origin story could be holding you back from being the best, most profitable business owner.

2. Reframe limiting beliefs. When you get to the root of your money story, you have the power to reframe those feelings and stop letting them control you. Literally say the opposite of your limiting belief ("I'm learning how to be awesome with spreadsheets" instead of "I'm not good with spreadsheets"). Double down on your self-worth. Break the link between money and your self-worth.

3. Create big, lofty financial goals for yourself. You deserve wealth and to be wealthy, so don't let fear hold you back from achieving it.

4. Face your fears. What are you most afraid of? Losing your business? We all have this voice inside of us that is constantly nagging us and reminding us of our fears. Understand that failure is part of business and remind yourself that taking control of your finances will contribute to success.

5. Act. You have what it takes to manage your money successfully. You are smart enough. Invest in yourself and take the time to learn these skills. Breathe and just take in all that is around you. You're doing a great job. Keep at it. Tell yourself that money can be fun! That positivity will keep you in a money-making mindset.

CHAPTER 3

UNDERSTANDING PROFIT VERSUS REVENUE

"What you focus on you create more of."
— JEN SINCERO

Tis is by far the most important concept in this book to grasp—*profit*.

Before we continue with the steps, there's something I want to make very clear, a distinction that will draw the line between the financial success or failure of your business.

You need to understand the difference between profit and revenue.

This is an area that confuses many business owners, and rightfully so. When you are short on cash, the solution is to go make more money. You just create a new offer and sell it.

But the thing is, it's more important to set up a money management system that will give you a solid financial foundation that your business needs to grow and make millions of dollars for you.

If you're bringing in money but always short on cash, you likely have a profit problem, not a revenue problem.

Businesses are in the game to create a profit, and you need to be aware of what you're making not only in dollars but also as your net profit margin.

Being a traditional business owner requires that you get familiar with terminology and business-speak. Your profit margins matter and they will be a key player in building the profitability of your business.

In simple terms: profit is the money that you get to keep at the end of the day (after taxes). It's what lines your pockets and helps increase your net worth.

But don't get me wrong. Revenue is still very important, but if you are bringing in revenue without profit, this is a red flag for your business.

REVENUE IS NOTHING WITHOUT PROFIT

It's a complicated relationship in that profit cannot exist without revenue coming in. But you can have high amounts of revenue without profit, and that is what we want to avoid. Sales are necessary in business, and the higher the sales number, the higher profit you will make if you are managing the money well in your business.

All too often, I hear business owners bragging about the revenue they are creating in their business. They talk about their multiple six, seven, and eight-figure businesses bringing in huge revenue numbers from launches and great marketing strategies.

But wait, are they telling you the entire story? Of course not!

When I hear a business owner telling me they reached seven figures (or whatever the number is) these thoughts come to mind:

- ✔ Are we looking at one year of revenue or multiple years?
- ✔ Do you have any profit to back that up?

To be a seven-figure business you need to make seven figures in one year. You are not a seven-figure business if it takes you three years to get there. If you follow traditional methods of business and accounting, which as a traditional business owner you should be doing, you will understand that to be truly considered a seven-figure business, you need to have made over $1 million in one year.

Often business owners consider themselves a million-dollar business when they have hit that million-dollar sales threshold, regardless of whether it took them three years to get there, or more. But what makes your business a million-dollar business is if you are making a million dollars of sales in one year, then revenue resets the following year to zero, and you have to make those millions of dollars of sales over again. Million-dollar businesses make a million dollars in sales year after year.

Another issue I see with business owners, which grinds my gears, is when they talk about building million-dollar companies, or multiple millions. Whatever the number is, it's important to remember that your profit and loss (P&L) statement resets to zero at the beginning of each new fiscal year, so to be a million-dollar business you need to be either making a minimum of a million dollars in sales each year, or the equity on your balance sheet must be at minimum a million dollars.

The next issue is profitability, and this is such an imperative part of business. You need to create profit, so going behind the scenes and breaking down the cost of generating a million dollars in revenue is vital for business survival.

When you start breaking it down and seeing the costs that accompany that one million in revenue, if there are no profit numbers to back it up, that is a red flag for your business.

You might be surprised to learn that many seven-figure and higher businesses go bankrupt because they are not profitable.

So please remember as you read through this book that although high revenue numbers are impressive, you need to have a money management system in place so that your business is profitable and will operate for years to follow.

I faced this situation with my client Amy, who was running a successful business and had reached multiple millions in sales in her business. She was very proud of that, and rightfully so, as it took her less than five years to reach $4 million a year.

When Amy got to that point, she was tired and wanted to step away from the business to spend more time with her family and friends and travel more. She hired a qualified business manager to step in as her eyes on the business.

She traveled, spent a lot of money on personal luxuries, and felt she was really starting to live her best life without a care in the world. She trusted that her business manager had everything under control back in the office and she enjoyed her time away.

But it didn't take more than six months for things to go south. She noticed her bank account balances in the business were not as high as she had kept them when she was running the business. She barely heard from her business manager and decided that maybe it was time to check-in.

Amy requested the latest income statements, balance sheet, and variance reports. When she reviewed the activity in her business, she realized that sales had dipped and expenses had increased since her sabbatical, and cash reserves were getting dangerously low. Amy was a seasoned enough business owner to know that if she didn't step back in and start making changes then her business would be at risk of closing.

Yes, it can happen that quickly. When your business stops generating profit, it affects everything, right down to cash levels. Cash is queen in your business and must be monitored carefully. When you run out of cash, your business will go bankrupt, no matter how large your business is and how many sales you bring in. That's why profitability is so important.

Look at profit, not revenue.

Sales revenue	$100,000
Expenses	-$70,000
Profit	$30,000
Net profit margin	30%

Profit = Revenue less expenses

There is a relationship between revenue and profit. Revenue is the money that your business makes when offering its products and/or services. Your profit is the money that you get to keep at the end of the day after taxes are paid.

KEY PERFORMANCE INDICATORS TO TRACK IN YOUR BUSINESS

When you're earning high amounts of revenue, but you do not have profit to back up those high revenue numbers, that is a red flag for your business. You need to focus on generating profit in your business so that you keep the business going for the long term. Believe me, in my twenty-plus-year career, I have seen many high-figure businesses go bankrupt due to financial mismanagement.

When business owners brag about high revenue numbers with no profit to back them up, that makes the revenue numbers vanity numbers.

Yes, revenue is important, and profit cannot exist without revenue, but proceed with caution.

If you are a business owner who is not making a profit in your business, before you start generating more revenue—which is the common response to this problem—look under the hood of your business and fix what isn't working. This is where knowing your business numbers is extremely valuable because your numbers will tell you what is going on in your business and what you need to fix before you start increasing sales.

I always tell my clients to have a strong understanding of how they create profit in their business *before* they start growing because that is what creates a strong financial foundation. You want financial control because if you start growing too early, you put your business at risk.

Now let's look at a key performance indicator (KPI) that every business should monitor. The top KPI to monitor monthly is profit margins. They are what I base the financial plan on.

What is a profit margin?

Profit margins indicate how many cents of profit have been generated for each dollar of sale by dividing income by revenue (profit margin = net income / sales).

Profit margins are important because they measure how much money an offer makes.

KNOW THE GROSS PROFIT MARGIN OF EACH PRODUCT YOU SELL

The gross profit margin calculates how profitable your product or service is before overhead costs are included. That's the cost of the direct material and labor that go into creating that product, and any advertising, shipping, and packaging that is directly related to that product.

Having competitive gross profit margins is essential for business.

This is important information to know because you will want to benchmark your gross profit margin against industry standards and know which of your offers create the most profit. Often business owners believe it's their bestsellers that create the most profit, but that isn't always the case.

The net profit margin takes into account all the overhead costs of running the business along with the cost of goods sold, and typically it is lower than the gross profit margin.

You want to be sure your net profit margin is competitive as well, and net profit margin should include all wages, including what you pay yourself.

You need to benchmark the type of business that you are in because all industries carry their own averages. For example, restaurants and bakeries typically have lower net profit margins at 8–10 percent, and service-based businesses are higher at around 50–60 percent.

A good rule of thumb is to have a 20–30 percent net profit margin if you do not know your industry standard.

Profit margins can be calculated on a specific offer so that you know how profitable it is. You can measure how you priced your offer, the cost of selling that offer, and how much money you make on each unit.

For example, Tammy owns a jewelry business and always felt her bestsellers were making her the most money. She knew that to say competitive and profitable in her industry she needed to have gross margins around 80 percent. When we broke down the gross margins of five of her products, she realized her bestselling item had the lowest gross margin of the five and came in at only 40 percent gross margin, while the other four products were at around 80 percent combined.

What could Tammy do in this situation? She had some options:

1. Increase the selling price of the product.
2. Decrease costs in the product.

3. A combination of both those options.
4. Heavily promote other products that have larger gross margins.

When you know your business numbers it allows you to make profitable decisions. By promoting other products Tammy had and turning those higher profit margin products into bestsellers, she could have increased her profit line. Or, by making cost and pricing adjustments to her existing bestseller, she could have continued to sell it with higher profit margins and increased her bottom line.

If an offer is not profitable, or not profitable enough, you can increase the price, decrease the costs, or a combination of both. It is important for you to have a decent profit margin so that producing this offer is worth your time and effort.

If you are selling multiple offers, you will know which offers generate the most profit and can focus your resources on selling those in order to make the most profit.

In the illustration below, example A earned $30,000 in profit from $100,000 in sales in year one. That equals an impressive profit margin of 30 percent.

That same business grew over the following year and made $1,000,000 in profit. If you just measured by those standards it would look like this company is doing fantastic because their profit increased by $70,000 from one year to the next. But looks are deceiving.

The net profit margin fell by 20 percent. You want your net profit margins to stay the same or increase as your business grows. So, following that reasoning, in year two the company should have made $300,0000 or more of profit from

$1 million in sales. Instead, the net profit margin decreased, and technically the business lost out on $200,000 of profit.

Does that paint a clearer picture of why monitoring net profit margin is vital to the financial performance of your business?

	Year 1	Year 2
Sales revenue	$100,000	$1,000,000
Expenses	$70,000	$900,000
Profit	$30,000	$100,000
Net profit margin	30%	10%

Profit = Revenue less expenses

Profit is the money you get to keep at the end of the day, and the higher your net profit margin is, the easier it is to generate profit from your sales.

You want to create high profit margins in your business because the higher your profit margin, the less hard you are working to earn profit.

Let's talk more about revenue and how important those numbers are.

You may hear this a lot: "Make more money." When you're short on cash, consultants tell you to make more in sales. Get another product out there, throw another launch, and just make more money!

But what does that mean?

Sales numbers can be impressive, and if you have managed to get your sales numbers very high, that's definitely something to be happy about. But when I'm looking for value in a company, that's not where I look. Sales numbers mean nothing without profit attached to them.

Regardless of the size of your business, if you are operating with tiny profit margins, at zero, or in the negative, the viability of your business will be questionable. And if you don't even know if you are in the negative or positive, you need to pay special attention to this chapter. Because this is where the money is.

PROFIT = SALES – EXPENSES – TAXES

Yes, you need to pay taxes on the profit you earn, and we will cover how to allocate a tax fund in chapter six.

That is the formula that you should pay extra special attention to because if you're the sole shareholder of your business, that profit is all yours at the end of the day. And you get to either pay that out to yourself or put it back into the business.

What would you think would be more valuable? A company that makes $7 million in sales but only has a profit of $20,000, or a business that sold $140,000 and kept $80,000 of profit?

You can bring in multiple hundreds of thousands in sales in your business, but if your bottom line is not healthy for your sales level, then it's a problem.

The value is in the profit because that is what is left over for you. It's in your pocket after taxes.

If you mismanage business expenses, chances are, potential profits are being eaten up.

Lately I am seeing a lot of online entrepreneurs bragging about big numbers. However, it's not necessarily as important how much money you make as how you manage it. If you aren't managing your money well, if you are overspending in your business and are left with little at the end, that's a problem you might want to look into.

A business cannot survive on good sales numbers alone. There are various factors that come into play, and the primary ones are that you control the costs of making those sales and that the costs of doing business do not exceed the income that the business is generating.

The key to maintaining a good profit margin when you have high sales levels is through good bookkeeping records that are accurate and timely so that you can run financial reports that offer you accurate financial information on which to base decisions.

The top six ways to keep profit in your business are as follows:

1. Focus on selling your most profitable services.

Many business owners don't even know what their most profitable offers are. When you know the gross profit margin of each product or service that you are selling, then you will know which is the most profitable, and you can spend more resources promoting that item. Your returns will likely be higher when you are promoting the offers that make the most profit for your business.

2. Trim your expenses.

Runaway costs are the most common reason for money leaks in a business. In order to be as profitable as possible, costs need to be controlled. Regular monitoring of your costs prevents budget overruns because it allows you to identify issues before they turn into big problems.

Often business owners fear looking at their business numbers for what they may find; however, I argue that the earlier you find out about cost overruns or money leaks in your business, the earlier you can resolve those leaks. The earlier you resolve those leaks, the more money you will save.

3. Increase your profit margins.

A profit margin is a ratio that demonstrates how much profit a sale leaves you before paying taxes. By breaking down the costs of each product or service that you are selling you will understand what drives your profit margin up or down. The higher the profit margin, the more money it leaves in the business. When you understand what factors are driving up your costs you can find ways to reduce them and keep more money in the business.

It's better to line your business with extra profit than another business.

4. Understand that each decision you make affects the bottom line.

There is nothing that doesn't affect the bottom line of your business. Every decision you make impacts your profit either directly or indirectly. When you understand how your business decisions are affecting your bottom line, you will make smarter decisions that keep the profit in the business. The best way to understand the profitability of your business is to understand your business numbers.

5. *Know your cash flow.*

Cash flow is one of the most important areas that keeps you in business, so monitoring your cash levels is very important. If you can't pay your bills, you won't stay in business for long. You need a good cash management system so that you'll know what bills you have coming up and if you have enough cash in the bank to cover them. This allows for proper planning so that if a potential problem arises, you can be aware of the fact before it stresses you out. Knowing your cash flow allows you to be proactive.

6. *Invest in your business.*

If you aren't sure how to understand your business numbers, invest the time in learning this skill. The return on investment will pay for itself many times over through the proper management of your business finances. There is no shame in reaching out for help. When you started your business, you did so because you were passionate about what you offer. As you spend more time in your business and care about the success of your business you realize how important it is to understand your business numbers.

There's one more issue I want to address before we move on, and we will cover this more in chapter five. Many business owners believe they should pay their salary with what is left over at the end of the month, also known as profit.

My argument is that you need to plan for a steady salary, pay yourself each month from your business to meet your personal needs or at year end you can plan for your business bonus (or dividend payment, depending on the structure of your business).

Savvy business owners know that they need to pay themselves a regular salary that they can depend on and that they can also draw extra if need be. But as mentioned several times in this book, be sure to discuss a tax-saving strategy with your accountant to implement the best tax plan for your business.

KEY TAKEAWAYS:

1. Understand the difference between revenue and profit, which will make a financial impact on your business. Revenue is the amount of money you earn through your sales or services; profit is revenue minus expenses.

2. Net profit margin is important to monitor in your business because the higher your profit margin is, the more money you are making in your business.

3. Use KPIs to monitor the performance of key goals and objectives in your business.

4. Understand how to maintain high profit margins for your business. The higher the profit margins, the easier it is for your business to generate profit.

CHAPTER 4

STEP 2: KNOW YOUR FINANCIAL REPORTS

*"Discipline is the bridge between goals
and accomplishments."*
— JIM ROHN

D id you know that when you manage the money that you have, it's an excellent way of making more of it? It's super exciting to think about it that way, and it's probably why I love numbers so much. I love money too! I also love teaching others how to make more money for themselves by showing them where the profit lies in managing those numbers.

Think about it in your personal life: when you look at and review your monthly credit card or debit card statement, you see where your money is going. It may inspire you to cancel that barely used subscription or help you recognize that you're spending a little too much on dinners out. Do you know your interest rate? Do you know how much you're paying in finance charges? Too many of us just pay the bill (or let the debit card speak for itself) and don't take that extra minute to look over the numbers. Knowledge is power, or as I like to say, knowledge leads to profit.

I came across a recent survey of two thousand small businesses conducted by Digits uncovered that most small businesses lack the financial visibility they need to be successful.[1] This lack of daily insight ultimately exposes them to short and long-term financial risk.

The findings go on to state that small businesses are struggling to understand where their money is being spent, how much cash they have, and most importantly, where they should be optimizing for growth or cost savings. In my experience, that is what my clients are experiencing. So why aren't they looking at it? Here's what I've heard from clients:

"Numbers are intimidating."
"I'm not smart enough."
"Why do I need to know this when my accountant takes care of this for me?"
"I'm afraid to see that I'm failing."

Likewise, too many small business owners fear their numbers and don't bother to take the time to understand their financial statements. In my opinion, as a business owner, this is one of the worst things you can do. Your business numbers

---

1   "Survey Finds Majority of Small Businesses Don't Know Where Their Money Is Being Spent," Digits, October 13, 2021, https://www.prnewswire.com/news-releases/survey-finds-majority-of-small-businesses-dont-know-where-their-money-is-being-spent-301399220.html.

tell you a story about how your business is performing. If you are not paying attention to these numbers, you're driving your business into the ground.

The most useful information you can get is from your financial reports. Your financial reports give you feedback on the financial performance of your business, and numbers don't lie.

Some fear looking at the numbers, afraid of what they will find. Tying too much emotion to those numbers is detrimental. The numbers tell you a story and give you feedback. They tell you the good and the bad. Knowing this feedback helps improve your skills as a business owner. It allows you to make smarter and more profitable business decisions.

All too often I have clients like Cate who come to me not knowing how their business is performing. Cate felt overwhelmed with work and hired another employee, bringing them in on a full-time basis even though she had no idea if the business could afford to hire them.

Cate never looked at her income statement and was judging how well her business was performing by the money she had in the bank, which is not an ideal strategy. Recognizing this issue, Cate and I got to work and mapped out their company's budget and crunched the numbers to see if it was a good idea to bring employees on full-time when the work could have been outsourced on a part-time basis.

Cate did see that she had hired too quickly, and she had to let an employee go because she could not afford to keep that person on full-time. She rebalanced the workloads and managed with the remaining employee, whom she could afford to keep.

The worst feeling is knowing you can't afford to bring on a new employee and then having to let them go. It feels awful. This can be avoided by looking at your numbers first before hiring to confirm that yes, you can afford them.

WHY YOU NEED TO UNDERSTAND YOUR FINANCIAL REPORTS

Part of financial savviness is understanding the financial reports in your business. You have to know how to manage your money well, both for today and for the future. You need to understand and apply financial management skills.

There are so many hidden messages in your numbers, and the key is to unlock this knowledge and use it to your advantage. You don't need to be an accountant to read your own financial reports.

You're a business owner. You might think you don't really need to know your numbers or that you don't need any sort of elaborate accounting system in place.

You are partially correct.

You are correct in thinking you don't need an elaborate accounting system, but you do need a system in place. Setting financial goals for your business and monitoring your financial progress is very important.

What I strongly advocate for small businesses that can't afford to keep regular contact with their accountant is that you need to learn the basic skills on your own. Even if affordability isn't an issue, smart business owners take a keen interest in their numbers. And if you do not understand yours, you are missing out on huge opportunities.

You don't need an accounting designation to make the best financial decisions for your business; you need to know within yourself that you are making the best decisions.

Nobody will ever care about your business as much as you do.

When you get familiar with the foundational aspects of business money management, it becomes as routine as brushing your teeth, and you miss it if you don't do it daily. It may feel overwhelming in the beginning, but you will come more familiar with your numbers and understanding the financial information in your business will become much easier.

When your finances are organized and you have a system in place, you can focus on taking your business in the direction that makes sense to you. Getting into a routine and following the Cash Confident Framework™ ensures that you develop a system for your business.

The methods I teach are easy and imperative for business success. They are essential in knowing your business. I break each step out so that you clearly understand what you need to know and how to implement that knowledge into your business.

As your business grows, you will likely have a need for an accountant on payroll. However, you will always need the basic foundation to understand why you should make certain decisions. So regardless of what stage your business is in, these skills will always be valuable.

The accountant provides a lot of value to you as a business owner, but the biggest value is in understanding your conversations with your accountant and other financial professionals—and not only in those conversations but all business conversations.

You will always know the financial health of your business and have cash on hand to meet financial obligations. When unexpected expenses arise, you will not panic because you will understand exactly how to cover these expenses. You'll be reassured knowing you have a cash system in place.

You will have a deeper understanding of your business. You will understand how to generate sales and get more profit margin from those sales. You'll know what expenses you can cut and how to grow your business. You'll understand the cycle of your business and break records of growth year after year.

These reasons and so many more are why you need to invest in the time to acquire that numbers skill set so that you are able to take your business to the next level.

When you learn to think like a CFO, you are considering the risks to your business and the opportunities available for your business, plus you see the big picture of what your business could be. CFOs are strategic thinkers, not just number-crunchers.

Business owner	Tax accountant
Oversees business finances at a high level	Reviews your financial reports to ensure you are in accordance with GAAP
Makes profitable business decisions daily	Completes your business tax return
Optimizes profit in the business	Advises you on tax-saving strategies
Manages your cash flow	

WHAT AN ACCOUNTANT SHOULD DO VERSUS WHAT YOU SHOULD DO

Accounting and reports are not the same as bookkeeping, and this is an important distinction to make. Keeping your books current and clean is the first layer of the financial foundation of your business. But taking those numbers and turning them into valuable reports—that's where the magic happens! That's why having a reliable bookkeeper is so important, because it is their job to record the data accurately. Your financial reports are based on accurate data, and that is what you are basing your decisions on. You do not want to have inaccurate books because it will cost you in various unpleasant ways.

You'll see how valuable bookkeeping information is to keep your business running smoothly. The statements are there to help you with money management. I know your business is important to you, so be sure to invest in the right bookkeeper.

What if you want to do the bookkeeping yourself or you don't have money for a bookkeeper? Make sure you know how to do proper bookkeeping. There are plenty of free videos on YouTube that teach how to do bookkeeping, so take the time to learn the skill and make sure you are using accounting software to record your books. If you can't afford accounting, there are some free options available as well.

Professional accountants go beyond taxes and bean counting. Do you know how well-trained professional accountants are in business skills? Accountants are the backbone or the spine of any successful business. We are analytical and strategic thinkers trained to understand what the numbers are telling us but see the big picture as well.

Accountants and CFOs take the big visionary goals of the CEO and support that vision through financial planning.

FINANCIAL REPORTS YOU SHOULD USE

Financial statements are an important part of your business because they contain valuable information about the financial health and viability of your business. The numbers of a business tell a story, and when you take the data of a company and run meaningful financial reports, when you understand what these reports are telling you, you will have invaluable insight into your business.

Business is all about numbers, so never underestimate the importance of understanding your numbers. The numbers will never lie to you, and they might tell you what you don't want to hear. But don't be afraid or shy away from them, because they offer you the most valuable information to help keep your business alive.

Financial ratios are used to gain a deeper insight into the performance of a business, but that is more advanced accounting, and for the scope of this book we will focus on the basic foundation of understanding financial statements.

If you have dreams of growing and scaling your business, you can't do that without the knowledge of your business numbers. So, let's get started with the basic financial statements.

Balance Sheet

The balance sheet is a report that will tell you the financial health of your business. It shows you a snapshot of all your assets to date, liabilities to date, and the equity that you have in your business for the date of the report.

The essence of the report is this:

$$ASSETS - LIABILITIES = EQUITY$$

The balance sheet offers a perspective and a quick view of what the business owns, less everything that it owes. The remaining value is the equity in the company, which can show the financial health of the company.

The equity can also be interpreted as the value of the company.

Banks and lenders often refer to the balance sheet when they are looking at how quickly you can turn your assets into cash, which is known as liquidity. Banks, lenders, and investors are particularly interested in your debt-to-equity ratio if you are looking for financing.

However, the top line of the balance sheet, cash, is the most important part of the balance sheet. Cash is the lifeline of the business. If your business runs out of cash, it will likely cease operating.

A burning question might be, "Why should I care about the balance sheet? How does that affect my business?"

A balance sheet offers insights into your business and how it is currently operating. I believe we can agree that the primary purpose of running a business is to make money. Not too many people would be interested in running a business that couldn't feed them. So, if there are signs of financial distress in a business, the balance sheet would show signs of that distress.

You use the balance sheet to understand the financial position of your business. It's not enough to just measure how your business is doing by looking at your bank balance, as there are so many moving factors in a business.

The benefits of using a balance sheet are plentiful, as a balance sheet is designed to guide management decisions. It's the custom way to report your financial position to banks, lenders, investors, and anyone who has a financial stake or interest in your business. A balance sheet determines the risk of your business defaulting on any loans or financial obligations, which can be of particular interest to stakeholders. The balance sheet can help secure government grants, loans, or any type of financing that it is seeking. Balance sheets offer insight into operational efficiency, profitability, liquidity, and solvency, which are helpful ratios to use when determining the long-term sustainability of a business.

Income Statement

Also known as the Profit and Loss (P&L) statement, the income statement is by far the most used financial statement in a business, in my opinion and experience. The income statement shows the profitability of a business over a specified time period. The time period can be measured monthly, quarterly, or annually, but when reading and interpreting an income statement, as with all financial statements, an important piece of information is understanding the dates covered in the report.

The advantages of using income statements are plentiful, and there are various ways to use this financial statement to your advantage. The income statement is loaded with financial data, which are gold nuggets of how the business is performing. I will show you how to interpret that information in later chapters.

Again, this financial statement is used by stakeholders, such as investors, bankers, and lenders, to determine how well the business is performing and how profitable the business is.

There is much diversity in the income statement. You can build an operating budget based on the income statement. You can determine profit margins from the income statement. You can use the income statement to make estimates on your tax payment installments. The list goes on as you compare historical data, pick up on market and seasonal trends, measure year-over-year growth in your business, and so much more. It allows you to identify your strengths and weaknesses in your operations. There will be budget overruns and high and low profit margins, and you'll know which offers are more profitable than others.

If you're not using your income statement in all of these ways, you need to.

Statement of Cash Flow

The Statement of Cash Flow demonstrates the money going in and out of the business and is typically measured on an annual basis. The cash management system will forecast six to eight weeks out so that you have enough cash in the bank to cover all financial obligations. We will cover cash management in more detail in chapter seven. In my opinion, this is the most underutilized statement of the three types of financial reports. However, stakeholders do see the value in them. It's important to note that the Statement of Cash Flow report is different from your cash management system.

The reality is, when you have a cash management system in place, you will not be using this financial statement as a reference point on a daily basis. Instead, you will have your own cash flow statement system that you manage regularly.

We will address cash flow management systems further in this book.

The purpose of a Statement of Cash Flow is to demonstrate the activity of cash going in and out of the business. This statement is important because it shows stakeholders how well a business generates cash.

The Statement of Cash Flow measures the business's ability to pay debt obligations and operating expenses, as well as generate cash. If there are risks that a business' cash will dry up, it will be reflected in the Statement of Cash Flow.

The Statement of Cash Flow also monitors the investing activities of a business.

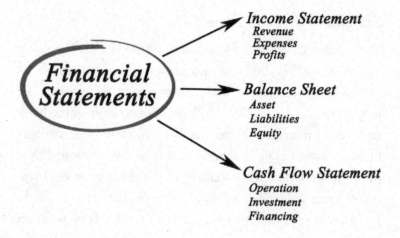

Income Statement
Revenue
Expenses
Profits

Balance Sheet
Asset
Liabilities
Equity

Cash Flow Statement
Operation
Investment
Financing

HOW TO MANAGE AND ORGANIZE YOUR FINANCIAL REPORTS

Getting into a financial routine requires you to know what to do and how to do it. It's great to know how to read your financial statements, but if you aren't implementing them into the day-to-day of your business then you are missing out on profit optimization.

Without a doubt, the P&L report will be the most used financial report in your business. The budget and financial plan are based on the P&L, which tells you how profitable your business is. It is essential to run these reports on a minimum of a monthly basis to know how your business is performing.

BOOKKEEPING AND BEYOND FINANCIAL REPORTS

Bookkeeping isn't just about managing your books to get your tax return completed. Good financial reporting is about optimizing the profit of your business. Profit is what you get to keep in your business.

But knowing how to create tax-saving strategies for your business and you as a business owner is financially beneficial.

When you run your financial reports and base your decisions on the information provided in these reports, it's essential to have accurate financial reports. When you start using financial reports and projecting your business finances for the next twelve months, three years, five years, and onward, what you are doing is planning the growth of your business and how profitable you can make it.

Profit is what you want your business to make because that is the money that you get to keep at the end of the day after you pay your taxes. The profit after tax will increase the value of your business, and when you own your business, it will also increase your net worth.

These are numbers worth getting excited about, especially if you want to be rich!

The fastest way to create wealth for yourself is through your business, and when you manage the money in your business then you are optimizing profit.

KEY TAKEAWAYS:

1. Your financial reports hold all the secrets to success. You need to review three reports—the Balance Sheet, the Income Statement, and the Statement of Cash Flow—at a minimum of a monthly basis to get the valuable feedback they offer you on your business performance.
2. The Balance Sheet tells you how much equity you have in your business.
3. The Income Statement (or P&L statement) will be your most used report and tells you the profit you have earned in the business.
4. The Statement of Cash Flow shows you where the cash was flowing in and out of the business.
5. You need a strong bookkeeper as the record keeping is the financial foundation of your business.

CHAPTER 5

STEP 3: CREATE A FINANCIAL PLAN

*"It's better to look ahead and prepare
than to look back and regret."*
— JACKIE JOYNER-KERSEE

In my opinion, the business plan is where the real magic happens. This is my favorite activity to do with my clients because this is where the transformation truly begins. Creating a plan for your business helps you see what you can achieve in your business in a year. A lot can happen in that kind of time, and you can take a business that is suffering financially and turn it around. Seeing where and how you will be profitable in your business is exciting for many business owners, and often there's a sigh of relief knowing they now have a roadmap to follow.

A business financial plan is a combination of where you are now and where you want to take your business. It is commonly known as an operating forecast. It is based on the P&L

and is a plan for the next twelve months in your business. You start your plan at month one, where you are currently, and by month twelve, it grows progressively to where you want to be.

Creating a business plan helps you to understand the ins and outs of your business. You learn how your business creates profit, what your most profitable offers and your biggest expenses are, the value of knowing your breakeven point, and how much you need to sell to achieve your financial goals. Creating your business plan offers you an intimate look at where your business is at and where you want it to go. Business owners who create financial plans and follow them reap these financial rewards.

Operating forecasts are not just for large businesses. In fact, I feel it is far more beneficial for business owners to create their financial plan themselves with the help of a business finance professional.

My top three reasons you should create a financial plan for your small business are:

1. A financial plan allows you to create a roadmap for your business.

   You are not only mapping out your monthly expenses, but you are also able to set a goal for revenue that you want to target for the month and the year. It also makes you very aware of your profit margins and what you need to do to increase them.

2. Planning keeps you accountable financially.

   When you know where you stand financially, then you understand the impact your decisions will have on the company. You are more mindful of money decisions. You know if you can afford to take on some debt and where you stand financially. You know whether you are on track or underperforming. There are no more excuses, and you are making an *informed* decision for *every* business decision.

3. Planning helps you keep on track with your goals.

    When you create a financial plan for the year, and you have income targets in order to achieve your set profit margins, then you can monitor your progress. You can closely monitor margins and fix money leaks as they occur. You have a better finger on the pulse of your business, and you can look and find trends in sales cycles.

A financial plan is a tool that measures your financial success, but if it's not monitored, there really isn't much of a point in budgeting. The budget can help you build growth into your business and allows you to see what is possible for your business.

When you know your business numbers, you develop an incredible sense of confidence as a business owner. It allows you to know your business intimately as you understand how your business creates profit and what you need to do in your business to create more of that profit.

Doesn't that sound exciting? I know it gets me fired up! Spreadsheets may not be a lot of fun, but counting your money is. When you begin to see how your financial reports are offering you feedback and helping you create profit, it just makes it more exciting.

Before you embark on creating your financial plan, there are a few things you will want to consider.

It's important to note again that your business plan is based on the Income Statement or the Profit and Loss Statement. In my opinion, the income statement is the most used financial report in your business and the most valuable. The income statement provides valuable feedback as to how your business is doing, so you really want to get to know it well.

A tip for when you start a business plan: take the data from the previous year and build on it. You can use the statement itself as your template. Keep the numbers you know that still apply, delete the ones that don't, and add new expenses for the year. The process does not need to be complicated.

First, let's cover a few basics.

PRICING STRATEGIES

A financial plan is an annual exercise, and along with it you should be reviewing your pricing structure. Prices often increase over the year, and the cost of your material and labor is likely to grow and shrink your profit margins.

Often small business owners believe that when the cost of producing their products increases, they should absorb that cost because they fear losing their customers. There is a mindset that customers will get angry and stop purchasing. But that isn't true.

For example, Linda has a successful candle business, but during this time of high inflation she has seen her supply costs increase steadily, as well as labor costs. The increase in costs has severely eroded her bottom line.

Linda's competitors were all raising their prices, and Linda had noticed an uptick in sales, presumably because her prices were lower. But she knew she couldn't sustain the lower prices.

Linda had a hard time when told that she needed to increase her prices because she felt that she would lose customers. When she realized that she had no choice but to raise her prices, she got creative about it.

When Linda raised her prices, she also changed her marketing strategy to show why her candles were a better option than her competitors'. She talked about how they burned clean, did not contain toxins, and how much fresher her candles are in the home.

The marketing campaign was successful, and yes, Linda did lose some customers. But she also gained new customers because she showed why her candles were superior to her competition.

Price increases can be challenging, but you need to raise prices on occasion to keep your business profitable. Remember that your business exists to create profit. It's not a charity. It is not the responsibility of the business to absorb the price increases and reduce its net profit margins.

I have many clients who own product-based businesses, and I teach pricing strategies to them. I have been there first-hand dealing with manufacturing, shipping, and rising costs.

Here are some tips to help you analyze your prices.

1. Look at your costs.

Reducing costs will increase your profit margins, so see if there are ways to purchase in bulk, make special arrangements with suppliers to get reduced prices, or examine efficiencies to save on the time it takes to create a product. Look at your packaging costs. Packaging costs are an overlooked expense. Is there a way to reduce packaging costs? Focus on reducing costs over presentation.

2. Streamline efficiencies.

When you focus on your bestsellers and increase the efficiency of manufacturing the product, you are reducing costs. You can save money in the time it takes to create a product. Direct labor charges can be expensive as well. Is there a way to make a product more efficiently, in less time, without compromising quality? Streamlining efficiencies is an effective cost-saving technique.

3. Renegotiate prices with vendors.

Your selling prices with vendors can be renegotiated when it's time to do a price increase, even when buying in bulk. Contracts can be renegotiated, and renegotiations are common, especially in times of high inflation.

Even if you are entirely a service-based business, don't discount the fact that labor costs increase along with the overhead expenses in your business. You must price accordingly.

THE MONEY MINDSET OF RAISING PRICES

We tend to get emotional when it comes to raising prices. You might ask: What if I lose all my clients? Who would pay that much for my product? Who am I to raise my prices that high?

These are money mindset issues creeping in. You can revisit chapter two if you find you are having issues creeping into your money mindset when it comes to price increases.

When you understand how much you need to charge for your products to make a profit in your business, it can help you combat that mindset and fear. Change is always scary, and you can't predict the outcome. But you also can't shortchange yourself as a business owner.

PAYING YOURSELF THROUGH YOUR BUSINESS

Another item you need to consider is how to pay yourself through your business. So often I see business owners who pay themselves with whatever is leftover at the end of the month. That system just doesn't work and adds more stress to the situation. This is not a way to build a traditional business.

You need to include a salary that you pay yourself in your regular expenses. Always leave a line item for salary and pay yourself at a minimum of what your personal financial needs are. Regardless of how you've structured your business, whether as an LLC or an S-corporation, having your business pay you needs to be included in the financial plan.

I recommend business owners also create a budget for their personal finances so that they understand what they need to pay themselves from their business.

Then, keep your personal expenses and business expenses separate. That means separate bank accounts, separate records, all of them separate. Make sure that you are recording every single business transaction that you have paid for your business out of your personal money through your shareholder loan account. It is very important to keep accurate records to leave a good audit trail, because as a business owner, the government may choose to audit you, and that is completely within their rights. As a business owner you need to follow accounting rules.

I have my clients go through their personal budgeting exercise first so that they know how to plan for their salary payments. This exercise is included in your free book bonus.

I'm now taking you through each step of the process so you too can create a financial plan for your business.

Step 1:

In month one you are going to lay out where you are currently in your business. This is a great starting point because this is where your business is at right now. You can start by copying the previous month's information into month one. You can adjust to accurately reflect the expected activity of month one if need be.

Step 2:

Before you start planning out months two to twelve, look at your business' current offers and know which ones are most profitable.

This means not only looking at pricing but also knowing the difference between your bestsellers and your most profitable offers.

Remember that you can't assume that the bestselling products are the most profitable. You need to know the gross margin of the products that you are selling to promote your most profitable offers over your bestsellers.

Then you can try to turn your most profitable offer into your bestseller.

Step 3:

Now that you have a clear understanding of the money makers in your business and you've adjusted your pricing as necessary, you can forecast each month, from month two to twelve, on where you want to focus your sales.

Growth doesn't happen overnight, so carefully plan out how much you will increase your sales each month so that your business can grow.

Step 4:

Ensure your expenses are increasing along with the increase in revenue.

Don't forget that it costs money to make money! As your revenue increases, so will your labor costs, costs of goods sold, advertising budget, and any other product or service you need to add or increase to support the increase in sales. Plan for that!

Step 5:

How are your profit margins looking? Monitor the KPIs that are important to your business.

I always insist that you look at your net profit margin when you are planning out your year.

Sales	100,000.00	10,000,000.00
Cost	70,000.00	7,000,000.00
Profit	30,000.00	3,000,000.00
Net profit margin	30%	30%

As you can see in the box, when your net profit margin stays tight, your sales grow as your profit does.

My client Maggie, who owns a beauty salon, was bringing in an annual revenue of $130,000 in her business, but at the end of each month her bank balance was at zero or she was in overdraft. She knew her business expenses weren't that high, so she didn't understand why she was broke at the end of the month. She wasn't even sure where the money was going! She thought if she worked harder to get that revenue in the door then all her problems would be solved.

What Maggie did was work harder, not smarter, adding revenue to her bottom line by working long hours at the salon and working alone.

However, the harder she worked, the more tired she was, and it really wasn't resolving her cash flow issues. She was getting burned out and she was frustrated that no matter how much more revenue she brought in, there still wasn't money in the bank at the end of the month. She was borrowing money from banks and third-party lenders just to have access to additional money. This was when she decided it was time to work with me.

We took a good look at her income statement and realized that although her business was profitable, she was barely scraping by. She wasn't even paying herself a consistent salary!

1. The first step we took was to break down the services she was offering and how profitable each service was. She saw on our spreadsheet that her most profitable service gave her a gross profit of $200 per hour and her least profitable service gave her a profit of $45 per hour. Guess which service she spent most of her time offering before she met me? If you guessed the lower gross profit service, you are correct.

2. We then got to work and created her financial plan for the next twelve months. We planned to bring in a new esthetician who would work under her and offer the lower-priced services. This freed up more time for Maggie to spend on her higher-earning service. When we crunched the numbers, we were not only able to increase the revenue that Maggie was making in her shop, but also, we increased the net profit margin to 33 percent for the year.

In one year, Maggie went from earning a 2 percent net profit margin to 33 percent, so not only did the changes increase her revenue, but they also increased her profit.

Maggie feels so much better now as a business owner and a mom too. She's able to take more time off from the shop, doesn't feel burned out like she did, and enjoys the freed-up time to spend with her kids.

Her quality of life has improved by the smarter choices that she has made in her business. But the thing is, she would never have known that all the energy she was putting into her business was focusing on the wrong thing unless she got to know her business numbers.

Your numbers don't lie, and it is about working smarter, not harder.

GROWING A BUSINESS

If you own a business that's planning for growth in the coming year, having a business plan is a necessity. Business plans map out your growth strategy and consider not only your expanding revenue throughout the year but also your expanding expenses. You cannot forget that it costs money to make money, so your expenses will not stay the same as your business grows.

You must remember that not all growth is created equally in a business. Growing too quickly can drain your business finances, so having growth included in your financial plan is a smart business decision.

You will need to add advertising costs, costs to create your offers, costs for expansion space, costs for hiring new team members, and other costs that can increase as your business grows.

Tracy Matthews is a jewelry designer who had a successful business before the 2008 recession. Tracy started her business in 1998 and made $50,000 in her first year. Her business subsequently grew, and as a result she had celebrities endorsing her jewelry. Revenues climbed.

In 2006–2007, she started investing heavily in trade shows and even had a QVC deal. But the trends in her business started to show that people were not buying as much, and taste was shifting. Tracy ignored these signs, and then the looming 2008 recession, dubbed the Great Recession, hit. The trade shows started to lose money. The QVC deal failed. She had to cover out-of-pocket expenses.

When the recession hit in 2008, Tracy was not financially prepared. She lost a lot of money, was not prepared for the decrease in sales, and had no cash reserves built up to help her weather the storm.

When growing your business, you need to look at your finances to support the growth. You may not be investing in trade shows for your business, but you will have to increase advertising costs, production costs, and larger cash outlay at the beginning before the cash comes through at the end.

It turned out that Tracy had to declare bankruptcy to get herself out of her financial disaster. It was a sobering time as she reflected on what had gone wrong.

Not one to give up, Tracy reinvented herself and her business model, and in 2012 started a new and successful business called Flourish & Thrive Academy, where she teaches jewelry designers how to run their own successful businesses.

Flourish & Thrive is a smaller business than the design business she had built, yet it is much more profitable and Tracy gets to keep more of the money through good financial decisions and money management skills. Tracy learned that you don't need expensive PR coverage, celebrity clients, and mass coverage to create and maintain a highly profitable business.

Flourish & Thrive is now celebrating its tenth year in business and Tracy plans on keeping on going. She learned from her past business mistakes and taught her clients what not to do from the lessons she learned.

Having a plan for your business, also known as having an operating forecast, is my favorite topic to teach my clients. There is magic in that financial plan because there is so much information. A business plan outlines the goals for your business and the roadmap to get there. Creating your business plan also offers you deeper insight into how your business operates and provides you with knowledge that you can only grasp by working through the plan.

Some people mistake the plan for a budget and hate the idea because they immediately think of "constraints." But business plans don't operate that way. They allow you to set sales goals and plan out what financial resources it will take to achieve those goals.

A budget, on the other hand, outlines how much revenue you expect to bring in and constricts your spending based on that revenue. It is very much like a personal budget for your household.

Budgets are great and absolutely essential, but in business I hesitate to focus on them because they limit the growth potential of the business. If you don't plan on growing the revenue in your business, then budgets are great to use, but if you are growing your business you want to focus on your financial plan.

The best part of the planning process is you don't just set a plan at the beginning of the year and then put it away. Good financial management has you monitoring this plan month after month. When you monitor, you can see where you are going wrong sooner, and you can easily adjust so as not to lose tons of money and time by waiting. We will cover monitoring your financial plan in the next chapter.

If you are not monitoring your finances (which we cover in detail in chapter six), you are missing out on big information and huge opportunities that your financial data is telling you. Numbers don't lie. Ignoring your financial data makes no sense to me because this is what you should be basing your business decisions on. The feedback you receive from that data speaks to the performance of that business.

I get it. When starting a business there are so many tasks and to-dos on your list, you often overlook your business finances. You must become a master of everything. You wear different hats as a business owner and can't really afford to pay the big bucks to the professionals.

The biggest task that I often see business owners ignore or move directly to the bottom of the list is accounting. That's because bookkeeping and record-keeping are often viewed as tedious, boring processes. It's the non-sexy topic of business management, which is ironic because money is sexy. So, if money is sexy, proper money management in your business needs to be sexy too in order to keep that money in your pocket.

I want to help you change your view on that and explore how fun numbers can be! Numbers are not strictly for dull reports that nobody ever reads or a means of completing your annual tax return.

When you understand how this can help you, you will have a better understanding of how you can take your business to the next level. You will be equipped to make smart business decisions, taking into account affordability, profitability, margins on your products and services, which clients are a money suck, and so much more. You can grow your business so much further when you have the right financial skills. Once you start understanding the numbers you will make better-informed decisions.

You shouldn't be in business to see what happens—you should be in business to succeed and thrive.

According to Investopedia, the official definition of a business budget is "an estimation of revenue and expenses over a specified future period of time. It's utilized by governments, businesses, and individuals. A budget is basically a financial plan for a defined period, normally a year, that is known to greatly enhance the success of any financial undertaking."[1]

Spreadsheets may sound dry, but when it's about money (more specifically, your money), what's not to love? I choose to think of a budget more simply as a plan for your business. It outlines your goals and lays out how you will achieve them—all by spreadsheet. There's no long narrative that you need to write. It's simply a page with a structured format and numbers, and it tells a story for those who are willing to read it. It's fantastic!

---

1   Jonas Elmerraji, "How Budgeting Works for Companies," Investopedia, May 16, 2021, https://www.investopedia.com/articles/07/budgetingforcompanies.asp.

Numbers and accounting reports are often overlooked, and from my experience, it is usually because business owners do not understand them. And that's OK. You are really good at the product or service that you are offering, and you make sales your focus. You likely specialized in your core offer in school or learned through experience. There likely weren't any business financial management classes when you went to school or when you gained work experience. If you did take a class, it was likely Accounting 101. And really, who loved accounting class in college? Even if you did, you likely only learned about T-accounts and debits and credits.

But financial management is so much more than accounting and bookkeeping. The real magic starts where bookkeeping leaves off. It's about running accurate financial reports and making smart business decisions from that financial information.

Building wealth isn't about the money you earn; it's about how you manage your money. Rich people know the secret that you need to preserve your capital and get to the point where you can live off passive income. Being rich takes a strategy. Being rich takes discipline. But once you know the secrets, you can do it too.

We'll touch more on building your wealth in chapter eight. Having that financial foundation in place before you start growing your business will help you increase your wealth far more easily with less effort.

You may be wondering, if creating a financial plan is so great, then why don't more business owners do this? My guess is they either don't know how to create one or they don't see the value in having one. But my money may be put on the fact that they've never even heard of one or know that they should do this.

If you are just learning about financial plans now and do not have one in place for your business, please remember that it is never too late to plan ahead. Financial plans can be created at any point during the fiscal year and should not be left up to chance. It's like the poet Maya Angelou said, "When you know better, you do better." Now that you know better, it's your chance to create a financial plan for your business.

When I first started working with Nicola, a dentist who runs her own dental practice and coaching business, she had no financial plan. She looked at her Profit and Loss statement on occasion but didn't really understand what it meant. She hired me because she was growing a multimillion-dollar company and knew that in order to get to that point, she needed to invest the time it took to understand her business finances.

She wanted to have a close look at her coaching business, where she coaches dentists on how to start their own dental practice successfully. It is a lucrative business and there is plenty of opportunity to grow it.

When growing a business, it is important to have your financial foundation in place before you start growing. You want to have competitive net profit margins so that as you grow your business your profit margins stay consistent or increase.

We created the financial plan based on where she was currently in her business and where she wanted to be twelve months from that point. Using the financial plan template, we reverse-engineered her financial goals (how much revenue she wanted to generate that year) and broke them out month by month.

Naturally, as her revenue goals grew, so did her expenses. We budgeted for two new salespeople on her team, taking into account when they started and how long it would take them to start increasing revenue in the business. You need to plan for paying salaries from day one and include any perks and benefits you are offering. A good guideline to follow is that it takes about four months for a salesperson to start performing. So not only are you planning their administrative expenses, but you also need to map out how much commission payments will be.

Other types of expenses you will need to plan for are increased office space if needed, increased marketing and advertising expenses, phone plans, travel, meals and entertainment, salary increases, manufacturing space, and so much more.

What Nicola noticed after doing the financial plan exercise is how many expenses actually go into growth, and how important it is to manage growth carefully. Not all growth in business is good. If you haven't managed growth properly and you experience a cash shortage due to bad planning, you are putting your business at risk.

In the financial plan template that I get my clients to use, there is a column for the forecast numbers, a column for the actual numbers, and a third column that shows the numerical difference. In the fourth column you have the ability to write text, and this is where you explain why there are large variances between what you planned and what actually happened. This keeps you accountable to your budget. There is no point in creating a financial plan if you are not willing to be accountable to it.

You will want to refer to your book bonus for the business financial plan template.

I recommend always tracking the current period and your year-to-date (two separate reports) so that if there are any patterns or issues arising, you are aware of them earlier rather than later, and you have time to correct any issues before they kill your business.

Being on top of your business finances is nonnegotiable as a business owner. You don't need an elaborate system. Most accounting packages make it very easy to generate these reports.

KEY TAKEAWAYS

1. Every business needs a financial plan! A business financial plan offers goals and objectives for the business to reach in the following year. You map out the revenue to earn, the expenses, and where the net profit margin should come in.
2. Your pricing strategy is an essential element of your financial plan. Understand gross margins and gross profit on each product and/or service you offer and reexamine your pricing annually.
3. Pay yourself. You are generating income in your business and need to pay yourself before the profit. The profit is what you reinvest in the business so that you can grow.
4. Not all growth is equal. You need a plan to ensure that while your business grows it is still maintaining or increasing the net profit margins.

CHAPTER 6

STEP 4: MONITOR YOUR PROFIT AND PROGRESS

"Beware of little expenses;
a small leak will sink a great ship."
— Benjamin Franklin

Creating a financial plan is an important step in your business, but if you are not monitoring your results against that plan, it's pointless to have one. Because you created your business financial plan monthly for the next twelve months based on the financial goals of the business, you need to monitor your progress against that plan each month.

The purpose of doing that variance analysis each month is to identify trouble spots in the business. You can examine what went well and pay particular attention to certain KPIs to keep performance on target.

When you want to quantify the data in your company, measure it with a KPI. They are used to compare results, evaluate business performance, and track changes to improve your business outcomes.

Back in chapter three, we reviewed the importance of profit margins. Profit margins are KPIs that are indisputably always monitored. However, there are many other KPIs you may choose to monitor, depending on your business needs. KPIs can involve strategic measures, operational measures, employee performance, and financial ratios, to name a few.

KPIs are important because they help align the business to achieve strategic goals such as profit, growth, performance, and sales levels. Numbers don't lie, and if you can quantify your key measurements, they provide objective feedback on business performance.

Monitor the KPIs, and if there is an area in your business that is not performing well or is having trouble, it is through observing the KPI that you can identify weak spots. When you can monitor your KPIs on a dashboard that offers a visual, it can help with interpreting data.

Mainly due to data analytics, there is an overload of data available. To make data helpful, KPIs help you organize and use the data and offer meaningful feedback on the business area that you want to measure.

You don't need to monitor every KPI, and the KPIs that you choose to watch will change over time. Your important KPIs are going to align with the goals of your business. When you use the KPIs that help you monitor your goals, it will help measure business performance.

I like to use dashboards where I can see all the KPIs that I want to monitor in my business in one place. It helps to have visuals and you can quickly interpret the results.

The types of KPIs that might be important to you to monitor in your business include the following.

FINANCIAL KPIS

A financial KPI measures the value of a business's financial results and performance. Every company should be monitoring financial KPIs such as profit margins. Profit is an essential part of business, and businesses need profit to grow and scale.

SALES KPIS

Just as essential as profit, companies need sales to survive in business. Sales metrics should be monitored, from sales quotas to new lead generation. Average cost per lead, number of onboarding calls, and customer acquisition costs are a few of the popular sales KPIs to monitor.

MARKETING KPIS

Marketing analytics allows you to track and report your valuable marketing KPIs for individual marketing campaigns. Social media conversion rates, landing page conversions, advertising, marketing distribution, and customer lifetime value are all useful KPIs to consider tracking within your business. Marketing KPIs must be monitored to see which marketing efforts resonate with your audience and which don't. Receiving that feedback allows for swift changes to achieve results.

OPERATIONAL KPIS

Used to measure the operational efficiency of the business, these KPIs help business owners monitor how effective the daily operations of a company are. When you watch your operating expenses, you can plug money leaks quickly so they don't become a significant drain on your profitability.

PRODUCT KPIS

Knowing the damage, waste, and return rates when you are a product-based business is vital information. Product-based companies typically have smaller profit margins, and it is imperative to monitor product KPIs and use that feedback to increase profitability.

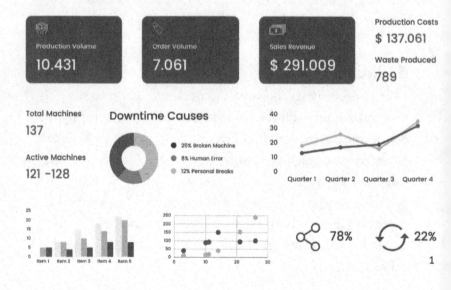

---

1   Erica Golightly, "How to Create a KPI Dashboard in Excel," ClickUp Blog, July 29, 2022, https://clickup.com/blog/excel-kpi-dashboard/.

The bottom line is that you can use the KPIs that monitor your business-specific goals. When you start using KPIs to watch for trends, you will see your goals reached at a much quicker pace. Using dashboards that monitor your most important KPIs allows you to maintain competitiveness in your industry. If you are not using KPI tracking systems in your business, you may be leaving opportunities and money on the table.

When you are building your business, keep in mind you will have various types of costs. There will be fixed costs, variable costs, and cost of sales.

Fixed costs are costs that are the same each month and do not change over time. For example, if you are renting office space, you will have negotiated the same rent for each month for the duration of your lease.

Variable costs are costs you can expect on a monthly basis; however, you expect them to fluctuate with usage. Common types of variable costs are heat, electricity, or cell phone usage. You know these bills come on a monthly basis, and you have an idea of what it should cost you, but you can't depend on the same amount each month.

Sales costs are the costs that are associated with a product or service. Known as the cost of goods sold or cost of sales, these are direct costs associated with the sale of a product. For example, if you operated a gift box service, the direct cost of sales would be the box, everything contained in it, and the price it costs to ship that good.

VARIOUS TYPES OF COSTS

Type	Examples
Fixed cost	• Rent • Loan repayments • Mortgage costs • Membership fees
Variable costs	• Utilities • Payroll • Consulting fees
Sales costs	• Marketing • Advertising • Production

Now let's review the steps you need to take to complete the variance analysis in your business:

Variance Analysis Example

	Budget	Actual	Variance
Sales	$100,000.00	$94,000.00	($6,000.00)
Expenses	75,000.00	80,000.00	(5,000.00)
Net income	$25,000.00	$14,000.00	($11,000.00)
Net profit margin	25%	15%	

Step 1: Run your financial reports.

Here's how: Once your books are closed for the month, run your variance analysis reports, and look at the variance between what you planned for that month versus what you achieved for that month.

A tip: if your accounting software allows, you can import the budget into the software and run a variance analysis. Alternatively, you can run the income statement and manually enter your results in the spreadsheet.

It's by examining the variance that you will get your most valuable feedback.

Note that if you are using QuickBooks for your accounting software, you can import the financial plan you created for the year. Once that financial plan is imported, you can run reports that show the variance right on the report. This is a timesaver, so you don't need to re-enter the data into a variance analysis spreadsheet.

Run a report that measures the actual results against the planned results (or enter the data into the variance analysis spreadsheet). The report will show the variance between actual results and what you planned and then you will investigate the variances. There could be variances for many reasons and knowing why those variances exist helps you in course-correcting.

Step 2: Monitor your revenue goals.

Always check to see if you have achieved your revenue goals for the month, as bringing in revenue is a critical part of running your business. If you fall short on revenue goals, it may cause cash flow issues in the business.

If you fall short on revenue goals, you need to understand why. Is it because you pulled back on your advertising costs this month? Or maybe sales deals fell through, or it could be just a delay in getting a deal signed.

A drop in revenue is enough to decrease your net profit margin.

Whatever is going on with your revenue, you need to be on top of the issue and know if you need to take further measures to correct it. There are many ways your revenue numbers could be affected, so take the time to understand the problem and mitigate any risks. This allows you to spend your time correcting the real problem.

Step 3: Monitor the costs in your business.

The next phase of monitoring your profit and financial plan is keeping an eye on your expenses and controlling your costs to keep your profits high.

It's important to monitor your business spending, especially in the beginning when start-up costs are expensive. It's easy to let cash run out. Many start-ups tend to be debt-heavy in the beginning.

You need to look at your expense lines and make sure you have stayed within budget for the month. When expenses are higher than planned, it eats away at the net profit margin, and it's just as important to understand what went wrong in expense categories as it is in revenue.

Did an emergency cost come up this month? Did you spend more in a certain category such as marketing and advertising than you had planned? Did that additional expense pay off?

Knowing the answers to these questions is important so you know what you are dealing with and if any risks will arise.

Step 4: Monitor the KPI dashboard.

One of the most important KPIs to track in your business is your profit margins.

It's important to know what your industry standard profit margin is so you can use that as a benchmark to measure your results against the competition. It's also important to maintain your profit margins or increase them as you grow your business.

For example, if you were earning $500,000 of revenue in a year and your profit was $100,000, that means your profit margin was 20 percent. Now if you were growing your business and you earned $1 million in revenue the following year and your profit was $150,000, you might be tempted to think that you did better because your profit increased by $50,000. However, that is not the case. To bring home $150,000 in profits from selling $1 million means your profit margin fell to 15 percent. Had you maintained your profit margin of 20 percent, you would have brought home $200,000 of profit. With your profit margin falling to 15 percent, that means that you have to work smarter, not harder, to create profit in your business.

Making decisions with only part of the story is risky because there may be a valid reason why something is happening. Maybe your revenue is directly tied to an ad spend, so if you stopped the ad, you would be cutting off the revenue, which is adding a consistent 30 percent margin per sale. Then it would not make sense to cut the ad. But if your marketing efforts have produced nothing, it may make sense to change the marketing message to see if those changes would help.

THE EXPENSE OF RUNNING A BUSINESS

I'd like to go into more detail about the expenses of running a business because I often see business owners get tripped up when they have high expenses in their business. Not all high expenses are a bad thing, and it's vital to your business's success to understand that difference.

Don't save money on the wrong things!

Running a business, especially in the earlier years, can create high demands on your cash. It's only natural to want to save it where you can. But I have seen too many save in the wrong areas and it bites them in the behind when they get caught.

Take business insurance, for instance. Business insurance is not only for brick-and-mortar spaces. It will protect you from errors and omissions, give you cybersecurity, and protect you as a practitioner from any legal action against you.

I see many small business owners forfeit the cost of business insurance feeling that it's so expensive and they would rather put that money toward something more important in their business.

The thing is, business insurance protects you financially. Your business is a financial asset that not only earns an income for you but has the potential to have value if you decide to exit and want to sell it. If someone were to sue you and you didn't have business insurance to help cover the cost, all your legal expenses would be out of pocket. And legal expenses are very expensive.

The reason you would want to set your business up well legally and insurance-wise is because it protects you from any financial pitfalls you might experience—and mitigates risk.

When you protect yourself from these types of risks you are protecting your business finances as well. Imagine if you were to be sued by a former client and had no insurance to cover the cost and financial damages of going to court. Or imagine you've spent years building your brand under the name you operate your business under (for example, She Means Profit™) only to find out someone else has been using your name and has even trademarked it. You've now lost a huge chunk of your business value.

LEGAL EXPENSES SUCH AS TRADEMARKS AND CONTRACTS

Having business contracts in place is important to prevent any misunderstandings regarding deliverables. Legal contracts protect you and your business.

Trademarks are important as well because you are building a business asset that people know and recognize. You're a brand that does not want to be copied, and trademarking prevents competitors from taking your brand as their own.

Companies such as Nike, Starbucks, Coca-Cola, and many others invest heavily in trademarking to ensure they own their names and others can't use them.

Smaller businesses, such as mine, have trademarking as well. I trademarked She Means Profit™ because it is part of my brand, I have heavily invested in it, people know me as that brand, and I wouldn't want any other business using it. If I did see someone using She Means Profit™ or the Cash Confident Framework™, I would have legal recourse to ask them to stop using it because I have trademarked it.

Now, I get it; investing a few thousand dollars in these types of things is about as glamorous as a house renovation getting a new roof. It's a significant chunk of cash for something that protects you but doesn't offer the glitz that a new marketing campaign would.

But I believe that if you protect your business now and something happens, you will be so grateful that you took the time to make those investments. Although these investments won't help you earn revenue, they will protect your business when you need protecting.

UNDERSTANDING THAT SOMETIMES YOU NEED TO SPEND MONEY TO MAKE MONEY

My husband understands the stock market and knows that if he invests a dollar today, if invested successfully, that dollar will not only appreciate over time but will pay him dividends each quarter. So essentially that dollar is working for him to make more money for him.

But when it comes to investing in my business, he sees everything as an expense. When my business launches a new program, I need to invest in advertising to reach potential clients. For example, I needed to invest in ad dollars to reach people I hadn't reached yet who would need my services. I had to reach people beyond my immediate network so that I could help more people know about this book and want to buy it. What my husband saw was a sunk cost. He did not see that for every dollar invested in advertising, I would get a return of an increase in business coaching and selling courses because I would reach more people who would want to work with me.

However, when it comes to investing in your business and yourself, you need to be wary of what others are telling you. It's a great sales tactic to manipulate you into getting that return on investment (ROI). So, when investing in yourself be sure that you will get the return that you are looking for.

I have a friend, Diane, who has been in business for decades, has a huge platform, and has authored many books but let parts of her business management fall through the cracks. She got caught up in the hustle and failed to invest in the activities that helped her generate more revenue.

Her excuse? It's so expensive. She has a fear of spending money on ticket items such as advertising or marketing that don't always meet expectations.

In business you do need to spend money to make money. As you grow and scale your business, some of your expenses will grow too. You'll need to increase marketing efforts, and as your revenue increases, chances are you'll need to add some team members to keep up with the demand. Yes, it can get expensive, but you need to look at the returns that these investments will offer you.

You may commonly hear the acronym ROI, which means return on investment. You may invest some money in marketing, and if you manage to double your sales then you have made a good investment. It means for every dollar you invested in marketing, you made two. ROI tries to directly measure the amount of return on a particular investment, relative to the investment's cost.

There are many types of investments you can make in your business. Another consideration is hiring a social media manager, as having a social media presence is important these days. Investing in the use of a social media manager can be costly; however, the ROI to be measured is twofold. One, with a good social media manager you have more free time to focus on revenue-generating activities in your business, and two, you will likely get the results of more clients interested in working with you because they have found you through your social media presence.

Podcasting can be an expensive investment to make if you are hiring for edits and promotion of the podcast. But you can attract many clients through podcasting, and it can be valuable for lead generation.

Investing can involve indirect everyday costs as well, such as installing a coffee bar in the staff room of your brick-and-mortar location, which may not generate revenue or attract new clients but could be seen as a valuable perk for your team members.

Sometimes the value of the return on your investment cannot be measured in terms of revenue generating but cost savings.

Let me share with you my story with Skye. Skye is a successful product seller and uses Facebook ads to help move her products. Her annual business revenues are $3 million per year, but when she looks at her expenses and profit, she wants to cry because profit just isn't there. She's still not making enough in her business to see profit.

She thinks because her Facebook ads are costing her 45 percent of her revenue numbers ($1,350,000 for $3 million of revenue), that if she wanted to increase her profit, she could cut back on her Facebook ad spending.

But that is wrong!

She knows that her consistent ad spending is the reason why she is bringing in such a high number of sales, so cutting her ads just doesn't make sense. She would just be cutting her sales numbers.

Just because her ad spending is high doesn't mean that it is wrong. This is why knowing your business numbers is so important.

The success of her ad spending is verifiable. Don't cut off the hand that feeds. You need to look at your business numbers more closely to determine what is really going on in your business to see where you need to cut.

As it turns out, Skye was in the start-up stage of building a second business, and she didn't separate her banking accounts for each business or their financial records. Although her first business was extremely profitable, her second business required more of a cash outlay and needed more attention from her. Once she knew that, she could focus on the issue and create a better cash management and record-keeping system.

Her confidence returned as she grew her second business into a profit-making machine.

OTHER TYPES OF EXPENSES

When hard economic times hit, the first thing large corporations do is look internally to see where they can save the most money. This strategy is common because, in hard economic times, your sales levels are likely to shrink. A proactive approach to declining sales numbers is to reduce the fat. In large companies, the first thing to go is people because payroll is usually their biggest expense.

If you're a small business with few employees, payroll wouldn't be the first place you would look to save on expenses. But the point I'm trying to make is that regardless of the size of the company, all companies will react by trimming expenses somewhere.

However, it should not take hard economic times for you to understand how cost-controlling works. Let's be proactive and control costs during good times and bad because controlling costs will help keep money in your pocket as well.

HAVING A GOOD ACCOUNTING SYSTEM

When you keep a good accounting system in your business, your financial reports will identify issues early in the process and help resolve issues before they become bigger problems, and you can plug money leaks into your business very quickly. Just by tightening up your accounting processes and procedures, plugging money leaks, and making cost adjustments and changes, you are ensuring you are keeping your business profitable.

When you see how these systems make your life so much easier and make your business that much more profitable, you'll wonder what took you so long to get these systems in place. These systems take a lot of stress out of running a business because you will be confident that you understand the business so much better.

When I was a controller at a telecommunications company, which is no longer in business, I was floored by how unaware they were of their numbers or profit margins. They had been running their business for decades, and it was during a time when pretty much any high-tech company was going to make money, guaranteed.

The operational budget for this company was $8 million and they didn't even have an accounting system in place. I just about died when I saw they were using Microsoft Excel as their financial management software. That is an inefficient system to manage the finances of an $8 million–generating company for so many reasons, and the top ones would be for internal control, accuracy, organization, and completeness.

But the purpose of this story is the fact that this company had about five streams of revenue coming in and they had no idea as to what each profit margin was. So the owners did not know if each was profitable! As long as the bottom line was profitable, that was all they cared about.

That is definitely *not* the way to run a business. That is running your business blindly. This company was bought out by a competitor in the end because it just refused to change its ways, and the money dried up.

THE BAD EXPENSES

Another cost to be aware of, or I should say, another money suck, is living the beyond-your-means entrepreneurial lifestyle. I see this a lot in the online business world, where there are influencers who are following other influencers and going into these lavish lifestyles. There are high-ticket courses, things like Mastermind classes, and in life before COVID there was a lot of travel to exotic places to conduct weekend retreats. Now tell me, is this all necessary to conduct business? Can you really afford this?

Chances are, with COVID, you are saving a ton of money and expenses on travel and meals out, and that should give you pause to think if the previous expenses were all really worth it. It's really important to control business costs.

Quite often business owners say, "Don't worry, it's a write-off," but do you really understand what a write-off means? It's still an expense, and if it qualifies as a business expense, then it is tax-deductible. That does not mean free. All that means is if you are making money in your business, your taxable income gets reduced by that expense. However, if you are operating at a loss, it won't mean a whole lot.

For example, when you purchase a $1,000 business expense, that means the cost of that expense will reduce your taxable income by $1,000 because that cost decreases your profit.

The most important result to be attained by monitoring your expenses is when you have a large money leak. For example, if you are constantly going over your marketing budget and the results aren't there, you can cut those costs. However, if you see the benefit to your budget overage, and marketing efforts are bringing in the results, then you can easily justify that expense.

Operational budgets and monitoring your performance against those budgets are very important in this area of business. We will be covering budgets in the next chapter.

CONTROLLING OUR SPENDING WAYS

A big question is how some people seem to manage their spending so much better than others, even if there is a planned or budgeted amount for spending.

The simple answer is that managing your finances is 20 percent knowledge and 80 percent behavior.

What happens if you have more of a behavioral problem than a knowledge problem? I will share with you that I fit into the category of over-spender, and it's a constant struggle for me to reign it in.

I get distracted easily by shiny objects and I tend to believe, subconsciously, that I can throw money at a problem to fix it rather than work on it.

The reason we are covering spending in this chapter is to help you have a better understanding of what goes into business financial planning and how you can adjust and monitor costs. This is an essential component to understanding how you can monitor your business finances and tighten up profit margins so you can make more money.

But on the other hand, remember that just because you have large expenses in your business does not mean that they aren't producing revenue. You don't want to cut the costs that are bringing in money effectively.

I want to walk you through an example so you can better understand what I'm trying to tell you. Let's have a look at Rosie's company.

Rosie is an influencer who is in high demand. She shares publicly about her multiple six-figure business. Her business offers an online course, she has a weekly podcast and a huge social media following, and she looks like she has it all. She travels to all the beautiful destinations, joins Mastermind classes, and lives the high life. That is what it looks like on the outside.

On the inside, Rosie is a bit of a mess. She pulls money from her personal and business account when she needs it and isn't very good at tracking her books. She knows that she's making decent money since her sales are so high, but at the end of the year when she filed her taxes, she was shocked by her tax bill, and even more shocked to learn that there wasn't enough money in her account to cover it.

How can that happen when Rosie's company is bringing in so much revenue? Let's have a look at her expenses. Because Rosie is not keeping accurate bookkeeping records, she failed to collect about $60,000 in money owed to her from clients. She paid about $150,000 in marketing ads to sell $240,000 in her online course, and she spent $30,000 to join a business coaching program. Traveling costs and fees to attend conferences in the pre-COVID days amounted to $25,000.

Rosie's Business

Course sales	240,000.00
Costs:	
Advertising	150,000.00
Coaching program	30,000.00
Travel & conference fees	25,000.00
Net income	35,000.00
Less what she failed to collect from a client	(60,000.00)

Cash balance	(25,000.00)

Can you see how Rosie overspent? It could have been avoided if she had looked at her numbers and controlled her costs.

The money leaks I've identified in Rosie's company are very common and easy to fix. First, she should have looked at her outstanding accounts receivable report, which would have told her there was a client who still owed $60,000. Then she would have understood that her online course's gross margin was $90,000, and her expenses were high for what cash she would have had left. When you get into a method or system of reviewing your financial reports and know what kind of irregularities to look for, you will be saving a lot of money and headaches.

It is very important to measure your business activity against the budget. This is how you will know if you are meeting or exceeding your goals. And if you are falling short of your goals, you will know why.

One common way to fall short of goals is by not meeting your revenue targets. The earlier you can identify these types of issues, the better it will be because you can correct whatever the issue is before it becomes a bigger problem. Bigger problems drain the resources in your business, and it is cost-effective to identify issues earlier to avoid big money sucks.

Another way of falling short of goals is higher-than-budgeted expenses. It is the same method as following your revenue. For example, if you have budgeted $10,000 a month for marketing, but you notice your ad spending is close to $10,000 already and it is only mid-month, then you are aware of the issue early. You can investigate the cause of this and decide if it's worth exceeding the budget for the month or if you should stop ads for the remainder of the month.

When you don't have controls in place for your business that will help you manage your expenses, it's very easy to get off track and spend excessively. There are advertising costs which take a huge chunk of the budget, travel expenses, course costs, Masterminds, hiring consultants and professionals to help you, and then your everyday business costs. It all adds up.

It's entirely possible for a six-figure entrepreneur to have nothing in the bank when they are not monitoring their expenses. I've heard stories of new business owners going into crazy debt to "look the part" of a successful business owner, which essentially means they had to have all the latest and greatest cars, vacations, technology, and so forth when they couldn't afford it.

When running a business, it is important to have direction. You need to decide what profitability levels you want to achieve for yourself and your business. Do you want to build wealth? Do you want to be in business for the long term? In what time frame would you like to achieve your goals?

When you plan out how you will achieve your goals and keep your expenses within a reasonable level in order to achieve profits, you will better achieve those goals and exceed them.

Rosie felt a lot of anxiety about her advertising costs. She was told by several other businesspeople that if she reduced her advertising costs then she would increase her profits.

Unfortunately, it's not as simple as that. For her, advertising spending is what generates sales, so if she cut her advertising spending, her sales would fall.

When we crunched the numbers, she could see that her return on every dollar invested in ads was two dollars. Those ads were generating a profit margin of 50 percent, which is impressive.

TAX PLANNING FOR YOUR BUSINESS

I love to help my clients prepare for tax bills. At month's end when you're analyzing your business numbers, it's a great time to see how much net income (profit) you earned that month and put a portion of that away for taxes. This helps guard against surprise tax bills at the end of the year.

But what happens if you do get hit with a huge and unexpected tax bill at the end of the year?

Before my client Emily started working with me, this happened to her. She had a profitable year and was happy overall until she had her visit with her accountant at the end of the year. She walked away from that meeting with a $20,000 tax bill. She had no idea that was coming, and worse, she had no money to pay it.

These types of scenarios can be avoided when you learn how to create your tax estimates. It's not an accurate portrayal of what your tax bill will be, but when you do estimates, it helps you plan for your tax bill.

It's your tax accountant's job to offer you tax-planning strategies for your business and personal taxes so that you can reduce your tax bill as much as possible. The tax accountant is also responsible for the completion of your business tax return.

At the end of each month, when you examine the profitability of your business that month, remember that all the profit isn't yours to keep. This EBITA (earnings before interest and taxes) is just that—what you have before you pay your taxes. The after-tax is what your business gets to keep, either as profit or to reinvest into the business.

When you estimate your taxes, you can safely put aside a portion of that profit that you earned for tax payments. Your tax accountant can provide you with a reasonable percentage, or my rule of thumb is to use 20–30 percent.

Your business tax rate is dependent on a lot of things, most importantly, what country you reside in and what state/province your business operates in.

Using an estimate will largely reduce the anxiety that you get when you receive a huge tax bill that you hadn't planned for.

If you overestimate your tax bill for the year, the worst-case scenario is that you will have extra money at the time the bill is due.

As a side note, I'd like to tell you about every business client that I have worked with. Clients come to me feeling overwhelmed and embarrassed. I assure you when you come to me, please know that I do not judge, and you have nothing to be embarrassed about. You simply have a problem that you need help with, and I admire people who can ask for help. That is a brave choice.

I am a CPA and I have education and years of work experience in corporate and personal taxes, but I would never say that I am a tax expert. I believe that to be a tax expert, you need to be studying and working in a tax environment exclusively.

Taxes do not bring me joy, and I no longer work in those types of environments. My sweet spot is helping with financial planning, money management, and business growth strategies. I leave the strategic tax planning and advising to my favorite tax accountants.

However, I do share tips on preparing for tax season, as I do love to send my clients to their tax accountant fully prepared. My colleagues love me for this!

Tips to help you through another tax year:

1. Stay organized.
2. Maintain a relationship with your accountant.
3. Don't be afraid to ask questions.

My client Christine knows the frustration of receiving an unexpected tax bill from the government. Christine collected all her business finance information and went to see her tax accountant at year's end. She had just finished her most profitable year yet and was so excited about the direction her business was going. She had big plans and felt confident about the finances of her business. It felt good to be finally making money. It felt good to pay herself dividends with the extra cash in her business.

When her tax accountant called her back to review her tax return and what she owed for that year, Christine was shocked. Her tax bill amounted to $15,000! And what was worse, even after her experience the year before with a surprise $20,000 tax bill that she could not fund, she had not set aside money to cover this year's bill, and she didn't have enough to pay it.

Christine went back to feeling like a failure. She was so disappointed and couldn't understand how she had been blindsided like that *again*.

What Christine had failed to do was plan for her taxes. The thing many business owners fail to plan for is the taxes they will need to pay on profit.

Profit is great and that's what you want to achieve in business, but you need to pay tax on that profit. And planning your tax expense is what you want to do.

So, at the end of the month when you are reviewing your results, make sure you take a percentage of your profit and put it away for taxes. Many use a separate bank account to keep their taxes in. It's best to keep them separated so that you don't get confused and think that money is there to be spent.

Through this chapter you have seen the steps to take in monitoring the monthly financial performance of your business. This is mandatory to do if you want to create a profitable business. When you look at your numbers monthly, you can see how well the business is performing in certain areas and identify trouble spots early so you can correct them.

When you correct trouble spots in the business early it gives you an opportunity to save tons of money that you can keep as profit rather than letting it leak out of the business.

Many business owners get into the trap of fear—being terrified to look at their business numbers and see that they failed at something. However, my argument is that failure only happens when you give up.

Looking at your numbers regularly is an ongoing process in your business. It helps keep you on track to reach your financial goals. This is an *opportunity* to make your business more profitable.

Regardless of what stage you are in your business you will meet new challenges. You discover those challenges by knowing your numbers.

Be the smart business owner who knows what is going on in her business finances.

KEY TAKEAWAYS:

1. It's great to have a business financial plan, but if you do not measure your progress against your goals then having a plan is fruitless. Monitor your progress against your financial plan every month.

2. Take steps in the variance analysis process and follow them.

3. Be sure to invest in protecting your business, which is a financial asset, from legal issues. Know how some expenses such as legal costs and business insurance are necessary to protect you from financial risk.

4. Sometimes you have to spend money to make money. Understand the differences between the types of expenses.

5. You don't want to get hit with a surprise tax bill at the end of the year. Plan for taxes.

CHAPTER 7

THE IMPORTANCE OF CASH FLOW STEP 5: MANAGE YOUR CASH FLOW.

"Revenue is vanity, profit is sanity, but cash is queen."
— UNKNOWN

Cash shortage is one of the primary reasons businesses go bankrupt. This certainly is a scary statement, but I hoped it grabs your attention, because it is true.

There is a difference between the cash balance in your bank account and the profit shown on your Income Statement. This chapter focuses on cash and cash balances, and we'll touch on why there are differences between your bank account balance and profit lines.

Cash management in your business is vital to business survival. That sounds harsh, but it is very real. Cash is what keeps the business going. If you run out of cash, you no longer have the funds to cover your business expenses. Suppliers will be very unhappy with you and will cease doing business with you.

You need cash coming in so that you can pay for things such as your rent and salaries for your team members, contractors, and yourself. It is a cycle that requires management and monitoring.

Having a plan for cash flow and proactively monitoring your cash levels will leave you with feelings of confidence that you are in control. There is nothing worse than being in a feast-or-famine cash cycle in your business. When you proactively manage the cash levels in your business, you can say goodbye to stressful nights worrying about how you will pay bills and where that money will be coming from.

This means doing away with short-term cash flow solutions, or what I like to call Band-Aid solutions, and instead turning to meaningful long-term solutions. But there are a few things you need to know about managing cash levels confidently.

Think of cash as the bloodline of your business. Without a regular infusion of cash, you will have difficulty meeting your financial obligations. You don't want to put your business in unnecessary trouble.

Cash flow management is important for all businesses, but it is critical for early start-ups. If you cannot manage your cash flow within the first year, you will likely not survive past the second.

When I speak of profit in business and how profit is essential to business survival, I have had some clients argue that cash flow is more important. The thing is that profit and cash flow work in different ways.

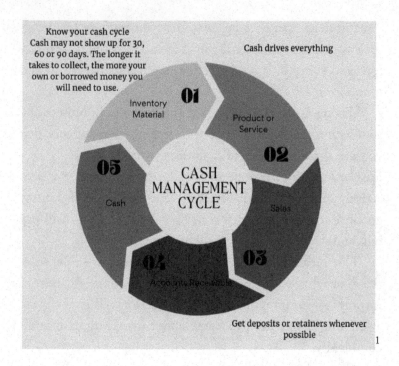

A business cannot exist without profit. Positive cash flow cannot exist without profit. If you are generating revenue but not making a profit, or worse, if you are operating at a loss, then you will be cash-strapped because you will need to keep your cash coming in to keep up with the payments going out. It will be a hamster wheel that just keeps spinning.

Therefore, completing all five steps of my Cash-Confident Framework is vital for money management. You can't just focus on one step of the framework, like cash management,

1 "Business Diagram Cash Management PowerPoint Ppt Presentation," SlideGeeks, https://www.slidegeeks.com/business/product/business-diagram-cash-management-powerpoint-ppt-presentation.

and expect everything else to work in your business. You need to implement all five steps.

As a business owner, much of your time is spent focusing on ways to reach your clients and help them—and that makes sense because the work you do is important. But the easiest way to increase profits can be overlooked, and that's by looking at your internal accounting structure.

If you're not keeping your bookkeeping records organized and current, you are wasting an opportunity to tighten your costs and increase the financial health of your business. When your books are current and set up well, you can run those numbers and get extremely valuable feedback on how your business is performing.

During downturns in the economy, declines in sales and poor cash management can cause financial trouble. During the 2008–2009 recession, banks tightened up on revolving credit and the kind of short-term loans that small and mid-size enterprises often rely on to get through tough times. If a business like that is over-leveraged or credit terms are disappearing, this is trouble. Owners need to undertake cash management analysis to address these issues.

It's not uncommon for the owner of a small or mid-size company to focus solely on the short-term cash management situation, but a business finance coach can teach their clients to take a step back and have an honest look at the cash flow situation and offer solutions.

Let's have a look at what you can do to cash-proof your business. When you take these steps to cash-proof your business, it builds up your cash flow system (and confidence) so that when you do experience cash shortages, you are no longer struggling to come up with a plan.

We will look at the accounts receivable and accounts payable terms, payroll, inventory purchasing methods, and how the current cash management system is monitored. Are there older-aged receivables that should be followed up on, new grants or funding that will be coming in the future, and is someone trustworthy in charge of keeping tabs on the cash balances?

First, let's look at how your bookkeeping is currently managed. When your bookkeeping is done on a regular basis, it makes it much easier to use your accounting system to run reports and make decisions off that data.

Bookkeeping needs to be accurate and timely, as it is the financial foundation of your business and what you base your decisions on. If you aren't keeping regular and timely records, you need to do so now.

Side note: I often have clients complain to me that their bookkeeper is behind, and they get their books returned months later than they want. If this is the case for you, you need to let your bookkeeper know you need monthly books returned promptly. If your bookkeeper can't meet your needs, find one that can.

When your books are set up with a good system, understanding your cash flow position is as quick as clicking a button to run your report. You'll know what bills you have coming up and if you have enough cash in the bank to cover them. This allows for proper planning, and if a potential problem arises, you can be aware of the fact before it stresses you out. This allows you to be proactive.

HOW ARE YOUR CLIENTS BILLED?

Point-of-sale (POS) transactions are common in retail environments and services where the customers need to pay upfront. When you have your business set up for point-of-sale, it's a great way to keep cash coming in the door quickly as the customer can't receive the goods or services unless they pay immediately for it.

However, if you are a business that needs to send invoices, this can be a lengthier process. This is common for business-to-business (B2B) services. This takes special care. The invoice-to-payment process can be lengthy, as you have contract requirements, milestone billing, and other considerations that point-of-sale doesn't have.

Often the payment is required within thirty days of the invoice being issued (known as "net 30"), which leaves you with a gap in cash.

When dealing with a B2B billing system, here are my top tips to help you get the cash from your client into your bank account quicker.

1. *Invoice your client immediately.*

Often, I see business owners invoicing a week or two after the client signs the contract to begin working together. This only delays your payment. You need to invoice on the day of the contract signing, especially when the payment term is net 30. The longer it takes you to invoice your client, the longer it takes to get money in your bank account.

2. *Offer discounts for payments to come in quickly.*

You can offer incentives to clients if they pay within fifteen days (versus the thirty days), such as a discount of 2 percent. You can arrange the terms however you'd like—this is just an example—but the idea is to give them a reason to pay you earlier. Many businesses will grab that chance to save a few bucks, especially when a 2 percent discount can translate into many dollars saved.

3. *Monitor your aged accounts receivable report.*

The aged accounts receivable report should be monitored regularly, which will show when clients are late in payment. Then you can follow up more quickly and prevent a late payment from becoming an issue. This helps with maintaining excellent client relationships and retention because your client will likely appreciate your organized and efficient follow-up rather than having a payment dispute down the road.

If you have a large number of accounts receivable, I suggest that you run this report weekly so no pending payments get lost in the cracks.

4. *Follow up on late payments quickly.*

The earlier you follow up with a client, the earlier you will receive payment, and you will avoid disputes over payments. The goal is to get that cash in the door, and part of your job is ensuring that you get it. The earlier you follow up, the less resistance you will get from your customer to pay the bill. The worst thing to do is to follow up with an outstanding payment when it has been sitting on your books for months. The longer that payment is outstanding, the slimmer the chances of it getting resolved. And the dispute might negatively affect your relationship with the client.

5. *Charge interest for late payments.*

If you notice that late payment is becoming a recurring issue, or you would like to avoid that issue altogether, set a late payment penalty fee that is clearly stated on the invoice. Be clear with the terms and conditions for payment. This will incentivize your clients to make prompt and timely payments.

6. *Maintain good relations with your customers.*

When you maintain good customer relations, your clients will prioritize your payments in order to not put the relationship in jeopardy. Personal client relations help you to collect payment faster.

> Tip: All too often I have seen businesses not reach out to clients to collect money that is owed to them. You leave money on the table when you ignore your aged accounts receivable report.

Running a business is hard work and often requires the owner to manage various roles within their business. Having a designated cash management person, if you don't have the time to do it yourself, will be valuable. Creating an efficient cash management system that others can follow will yield not only positive cash balances but also happy customers who are not disputing with you over unpaid bills.

For some it can be difficult to collect payment from a client, but I need to reinforce this: the longer you wait to contact your client about outstanding payments, the harder it will be to collect the payment. When you follow up promptly, it's fresh in the client's mind and they can pay immediately.

My client Kelly is a consultant and had a client who hadn't paid their bill. It was overdue by four months before she realized it, and instead of contacting her client directly she contacted a lawyer to help her collect her money.

That was a costly approach in collections in that she paid the lawyer for their time and she also offended her client. Remember, these are valuable clients who want to be treated as such.

We've spent much time looking at how you can get that cash in the door quickly. Now let's look at your responsibility as a business owner to pay your financial obligations and what you can do to save money.

SAVE MONEY ON LATE PAYMENTS.

Keeping current books means you know what payments are due when and you manage your cash flow so you have the cash to pay the bills when they're due. This saves a lot of money on late fees and interest charges. Your suppliers will value you as a good client and often offer benefits or discounts for preferred clients. If you're in a pinch and need special attention from them, they'll help you out happily.

According to Sage, which is an accounting software for small businesses, one in ten invoices are paid late, resulting in a global impact of $3 trillion.[2]

2   Johanna Brown-Lyons, "Late payments: Why your invoices are delayed and how to get them paid faster," Sage Advice, December 7, 2019, https://www.sage.com/en-us/blog/late-payments-get-paid-faster/.

IDENTIFY THE MONEY LEAKS BEFORE THEY BECOME A BIG PROBLEM.

When your books are current, you can see where you are spending more on a service than you intended. Marketing is typically a large expense, so keeping current records allows you to monitor the dollars you've spent there and helps you manage your budget accordingly. Running regular reports allows you to determine earlier when you are spending too much on a certain expense in your business.

CHECK OUT THE FORECAST AND VARIANCE ANALYSIS PROCESS.

The client should have, at minimum, an annual operating budget set up. Ideally, we would like to see the annual budget set up and frozen at the beginning of the year, and monthly forecasts adjusted with month-end variance analysis conducted. This gives the owner an excellent understanding of the direction in which the company is heading.

> Tip: Cash balances do not mean that money is there to spend. Cash management goes beyond that to ensure you have future cash balances to cover your financial needs.

CASH MANAGEMENT IS CRUCIAL FOR PRODUCT-BASED BUSINESSES.

When you are a product-based business you experience more cash management challenges than a service-based business, and that's because your cash demands come at the start of the cycle, and you receive the cash injection once your product is sold.

Before you even reach your first sale you spend money on setting up your business, finding a manufacturer, testing your product, creating your product, and then finally selling it. It requires a lot of cash outlay for product-based businesses.

To look at your expenses and get scared by big numbers does not mean that those numbers are bad. There are cost-effective choices you can make, but on the whole, you need to invest in your business to either sustain it or grow it.

I realize there are a lot of gurus out there who talk about starting a business for as little as $200, but if you are serious about your business and you choose to go into business to support the lifestyle of your choice, the harsh reality is you need to pay bills, especially in the beginning when a lot of cash is going out the door.

HAVING A FEW FUNDAMENTALS IN PLACE FOR YOUR BUSINESS AND BANKING

Now we're going to look at what you need to set up and keep ongoing in your business to support your cash management.

All businesses experience cash shortfalls at some time. I recommend you have a cash reserve that can pull you through a three to six–month operating period. This cash reserve is often referred to as an emergency fund and you are responsible for saving up for this. It is a cushion to help you get through difficult times.

You may be screaming at me right now and saying there is no way you can spare that kind of cash in your business right now. I get it, and it's a goal that you will progressively work toward over time.

This amount of working capital can help get the business through a market downturn or a difficult period in the business. It will also take away the worry of a cash shortage.

It is also time to consider a Plan B for cash reserves if and when you experience cash shortages. Setting up lines of credit and business loans with a bank is smart to consider.

> Tip: Set up a line of credit with your bank in good times, when the bank is likely to accept your application, and you'll have the credit ready to support you through the harder times. If you wait until you really need the line of credit, you face a risk of refusal.

Now let's put all these pieces together to see how you can proactively monitor your day-to-day cash levels.

If you are using accounting software like QuickBooks, you can run cash management reports at the click of a button. Cash management reports are a handy tool as they automatically lay out your cash balance, all the money you expect to have coming in, and all the money that is expected to go out during the specified time frame.

Having a report that you can generate just like that is such a time saver. Otherwise the alternative is to do it manually.

If you generate this report regularly you will see if you have the cash levels in your bank account to cover your cash commitments. If the report shows that you are short on cash, you can rest easy because you have Plan B in place where you can use either your emergency fund or line of credit to help you through the cash shortage.

There are many benefits to effective cash management, which include less stress, confidence in knowing that you will be able to meet your financial obligations, and an understanding of when payments from clients will be arriving in your bank account. Having a cash management system in place minimizes risk against your business.

> Tip: Using accounting software like QuickBooks that has all your accounting needs embedded into the program is a time saver worth any extra expense it may cost!

CASH RESERVES IN THE BUSINESS

A good rule of thumb is to have cash on hand to help get the business through a slower economic time or cash-timing issues. Building up these reserves can be challenging for some businesses, especially when you require a lot of cash upfront to purchase supplies and products.

Building a cash reserve, which is also known as an emergency fund, is smart for business. You would want to create a reserve that would last you six months of expenses. For example, if you have approximately $10,000 of expenses each month, you would want to save a cash reserve of approximately $60,000. These reserves help you meet short-term financial gaps or cover any emergency expenses in the business.

The cash reserve can be parked in a high-interest savings account so that you can earn the maximum amount of interest possible without investing the money. The money needs to be liquid, which means you need to have quick and easy access to it.

Any excess cash above the required cash reserve/emergency fund should be invested in longer-term and higher-return investment vehicles, such as stocks, bonds, rental properties, or whatever type of investment suits your needs.

> Tip: When investing excess cash in the business, it is best to get individualized tax-saving advice. Everyone has a unique tax plan and what is recommended for your neighbor may not suit your individual needs.

GOOD DEBT VERSUS BAD DEBT IN BUSINESS

Not all debt is created equally, or so some experts say. It is not uncommon to hear that there is good debt to be had in business. Many feel that if you are borrowing money to make money, then it is considered to be good debt.

I'm of the opinion that debt is debt, good or bad.

Personally, I feel when you start to rationalize debt by calling it good, you are walking on thin ice. You can justify pretty much any debt in your business when you look at it that way, which is why I prefer not to blur the lines.

Don't forget that when you borrow money, you want to be cognizant of how much borrowing money will cost. Interest rates aren't as cheap as they used to be (note that I am writing this book in 2022 when interest rates are currently rising quickly).

I like the alternative, which is bootstrapping. When you are bootstrapping your business, you are cost-aware, and you only pay for business expenses that you have the cash for as you can afford them.

I know it's tempting to have the best of everything at the beginning for clients to take you seriously. But that is a fast track to over-leveraging yourself. Be aware that growing your business too quickly can also pose a risk to the business if the current structure is not set up for growth success. Understand what is more important to you—growth versus profits is key in helping you to set up your business for success. Managing your debt levels and ensuring you stay within a "safe" level of debt is essential. Let's examine those levels now.

DEBT RATIOS AND OVER-LEVERAGING

All debt is debt, and when your business is over-leveraged, it will not matter to collectors that you have good debt versus bad debt. Be careful how much you leverage your business and watch those debt ratios.

DEBT RATIO = TOTAL DEBT / TOTAL ASSETS

In general, many investors look for a company to have a debt ratio between 0.3 and 0.6, and anything over 0.6 (or 60 percent) is considered high and likely would not qualify for further financing.

It's not uncommon for business owners to use their own funds to infuse cash into their businesses. Finding funding from banks or other sources is extremely difficult during the start-up phase as the banks are not likely prepared to take risks on small businesses.

When you are using personal debt to fund business activities, be sure to keep good records that clearly support that the money was used for the business, and make sure the business pays you back when it can.

Also remember to have a debt repayment plan if you are in debt. Often people borrow money without taking into consideration how that money will be repaid.

TAX PAYMENTS

Paying taxes is an inevitable part of doing business. In chapter six, where we talked about monitoring your progress against your financial goals, I also outlined the importance of saving money for tax payments. You calculate a percentage of your profit and put that money away for tax payments.

I suggest putting tax payments into a separate bank account so that you have the money set aside and you don't risk confusion on it and think that money is there to spend in the business.

Planning for taxes is important because you want to be sure that you can meet your tax commitments and avoid any penalties and late charges for late submissions. Those costs are completely avoidable.

I have a client named Ella who didn't pay much in taxes in her first year of business because she didn't make a lot of profit. But in her second year of business, she had a great year. Business was picking up and she made a lot in profit. She loved the traction she was getting in her business and started spending more money. But there was a critical mistake she made....

She failed to cash-manage and didn't plan for taxes. It completely eluded her that the profit she was making was taxable and that her business would owe taxes at the end of the year.

Before she was aware of her tax bill, she spent money on an expensive vacation and other luxuries to celebrate all the successes that she had had in the year. She lived large and felt really good.

Then the hammer dropped after her visit to her tax accountant's office to pick up her tax return. She was floored to discover that she had a $30,000 tax bill! How did this happen?

Failing to plan for taxes and putting that money aside to pay your tax bill at the end of the year will cause unnecessary stress for you. So please heed the advice I am giving you—always tax plan! You don't want to be in the same position as Ella.

I also have a client named Wendy, who made $2 million in revenue in one year, and yet her bank balance was consistently overdrawn. She had several projects on the go but had no idea of the profitability of each one. Her main source of revenue was consistent, but she had failed to consider the cost of what each project was losing.

Because Wendy was unaware of the losses she was incurring, she never thought to create a plan for profitability for her new projects.

Wendy just kept going month to month, incurring approximately $2,000 per month in interest and bank charges for overdrawn funds. She would never get ahead and kept wondering why this was happening. It was so frustrating for her because she knew she was making really good money, yet she was broke.

It was through creating that financial plan for her main business that she started realizing that she needed a solid financial plan for her additional projects.

When you start a business, much of your profit goes back in to fund its growth. This growth stage is extremely important, so cash management is key. You want to create as much profit as possible and manage your cash flow.

Sam, a successful book author and business owner, decided to start her own publishing company, but she was not taking into account that she was starting a new business that was draining her other business's cash flow. She had forgotten how much money was involved with starting a new business and took for granted that her other business was profitable. She wasn't monitoring the spending for her new business and didn't realize how her main business was funding these new activities. She didn't scale back spending because she failed to recognize that she needed to bootstrap her new business. The two businesses were not at the same stage in the profit cycle.

So, we created a new business finance plan that included both businesses operating as one to ensure that while she was operating both businesses she was monitoring her costs and net profit margin. She didn't want to go broke starting her publishing company, so we took that into account.

OK, so you've taken all my tips into consideration at this point. You've worked on your money mindset to bring in profit to your business, you've learned how to read your financial statements, you've done your business financial planning and monitoring, and you are managing your cash well.

You've seen a huge improvement in your finances and are happy that you are no longer struggling with the cash levels in your business. Now what?

This is where you can diversify investments and start wealth building. Once you have your cash reserve built up, you want to start investing the excess money and get it working for you. Getting your money working for you is a healthy part of building your wealth.

Cash management is more habit-forming than anything, and once you have a good system down with a solid understanding as to why you are doing it, then the rest is easy.

Now we enter the second part of the book, where we really understand what it is you can do to become rich! It's time to grow your net worth.

KEY TAKEAWAYS:

1. Cash is queen in your business. When you run out of cash to pay your financial obligations, your business will cease to exist.

2. Cash management is a system that you need in place to proactively monitor cash levels and ensure you don't fall below your cash management threshold.

3. Debt is debt. Some experts say that there is good debt and bad debt. Bad debt keeps you trapped in a borrowing cycle with high-interest fees. The goal should be to limit all kinds of debt.

4. Always be prepared for hidden business costs, expenses, and major setbacks. Keep cash aside to cover your tax bill and for any emergency or unexpected costs.

CHAPTER 8

BUILD YOUR WEALTH

"If you don't build your dreams, someone will hire you to help build theirs."
— Tony Gaskins

Have you ever had that feeling that you were meant for more? What did you do about it? Did you pursue it? Or did it scare you?

I always knew I was meant for more in my career. I knew back in 2004 with absolute certainty that I wanted to start my own business, and I also knew with absolute certainty that I would end up offering business finance coaching for small business owners.

Yet, I let fear overcome me. In 2013 I made a less-than-stellar effort to start a side hustle—I created a website and waited for people to come to me. Obviously, that was no strategy for potential clients to even find me. So, I stayed at jobs that weren't a great fit for me, I endured the corporate lifestyle, and I remained unhappy.

When you aren't pursuing what truly makes you happy, you are holding yourself back from greatness. You may consciously make the decision not to pursue these whispers in your soul telling you that you want more until they come in so loud that they are screaming at you to listen.

I've been there. What I learned through that experience is that it's always counterproductive to try to silence those whispers even though it feels easier to ignore them and live in fear of stepping out of your comfort zone. We just can't bury those feelings without them popping up somewhere else.

You were meant for more than that.

The same goes for building your wealth. You may have this voice inside you that says you are meant for more and that getting out of debt and learning how to live a better, happier, wealthier life is important to you. You're tired of feeling trapped in debt and you're tired of the stress and discomfort it causes you. You are just plain tired of it all, and the stress is eating away at your soul.

Money causes a vast array of emotions. We need money; it makes the world go round. Can you even think of many activities that don't involve money? Money is the world-wide accepted currency that helps you fill your needs and your wants.

Whether you are carrying extra debt or not, you may be holding yourself back in other ways. Maybe you are holding back on creating wealth for yourself by not starting that personal financial plan. Maybe you are not growing your business.

Money mindset is real, and it can be an issue that you need help working through. Objections to getting help flood us because the brain wants to protect us from change. You don't have enough time; it's too expensive, she's overcharging, she's ripping me off, I don't really need that, I can do it myself...the list of excuses goes on.

But what you are really objecting to is the fear of change. What if I fail? What if I succeed? What if I actually manage to pull myself out of debt? That stuff is the scary stuff. That's what's holding you back. It's never about the money. It's always about the emotions.

Change is hard. Change takes work. But what's worse than change? Staying stuck.

When you cross over to get to the other side of the fear, it feels amazing. And the possibilities and opportunities for yourself are endless.

So, do you want to stay stuck?

Now that you have been given the tools and resources you need to manage the money in your business so that you are making tons of profit with high net profit margins in your business, we still have a little bit more work to do.

You need to focus on the personal side of your finances.

It's been my experience when I work with business owners that the personal side of their financial situation needs just as much work as the business side. No judgment from me; it's just a fact!

I want to reiterate the importance of managing the finances of your business well. As a small to medium–size business owner, chances are that you own 100 percent of your business, so that business is a financial asset for you. The higher the equity in your business, the higher your personal net worth will be.

When you are building your wealth, it's not how much money you bring in that makes you wealthy. It's not the seven or eight-figure revenue, it's not the successful launch of a new product, and it certainly isn't the celebrity status. The secret to wealth is how you manage your money. This is an essential fact that you need to understand about getting wealthy.

That sounds like more work, right? It may sound lackluster or feel like a bit of a letdown. You've come this far and maybe you wanted to hear that luxury yachts are where it's at! They might be, but you still need a strategy to afford that type of lifestyle, and it's going to require more planning to get there.

There are rules for personal wealth management that you need to follow regardless of how much money you are bringing in. These rules are included below.

LIVE WITHIN YOUR MEANS

Even millionaires need to live within their means. It's only human nature to want more of what we don't have, so you might always be craving the next best thing in your life. Some like to focus on material things that they want to attain, and that's totally OK if they can afford it.

The misconception about having a lot of money is that it will always flow in. It can if you plan that way. You still need to manage the money you have coming in, live within your means, and have as little debt as possible.

The thing about money flowing in is that it isn't always a sure thing. That's why you always need to monitor your finances. That's why it is often referred to as financial fitness—you need to maintain this for life, and it takes work and a healthy routine.

The best way to be sure that you are living within your means is to create a budget. Knowing how much money you have coming in each month and making sure that your monthly expenses don't exceed that incoming money is living within your means.

RICH PEOPLE INVEST THEIR MONEY

I always encourage my clients to have more than one revenue stream. What does that mean? It means creating various ways to bring in money, such as different offers for your clients, passive income streams, and so on, so that you can protect your business.

This is called income diversification. As market conditions fluctuate, when you have a stronger performing income stream that starts to fizzle, you will have other income streams that are still running and can protect you through the tougher times. This is a smart strategy that mitigates risk.

When you have larger investment portfolios, it may be time to bring on the professional guidance and advice of a certified financial planner if you haven't done so already.

I advise going with a fee-based planner rather than a planner who gets compensated through the commission on the products they sell you. Use a financial advisor who has tax experience in your area, as you will save a lot of money through tax-saving strategies as well. Your financial advisor will know if it's best to keep your investments within the business, a holding company, or personally.

Regardless of where you keep your investments, you will need to invest your money and build on your capital. Rich people know to invest their cash and live off the income that their investments generate. This way, you are preserving your capital and can enjoy the finer things in life with your investment revenue.

Another secret of the wealthy is to diversify investments. Market conditions are continually changing, and demand for one product or service will fluctuate over time. Having other sources of income coming from various investments will help offset the negative consequences of market fluctuations.

Here are four suggestions for different types of passive income you can bring into your personal portfolio:

Rental revenue
Angel investing
Stock market shares
Bonds

These are some examples of different types of passive income streams that you can have in your investment portfolio, but they aren't the only ones. You can get as creative as you'd like.

I do caution you about passive investing. The word *passive* suggests that there is a limited effort on your part, and I tend to disagree. Passive income isn't really passive; it still requires you to be involved and monitor performance. You may not have to do much to generate income, but you need to be involved in the management of that income and your portfolio.

Active income is the income that you are generating in your business through the goods and/or services that you offer.

You should consult a finance professional who can advise you on the best place to invest—whether that be through your business or in your personal investment portfolio. Tax savings strategies are worth exploring because they will save you a lot of money in the long run.

A note I'd really like to emphasize is that even if you have financial planners and tax accountants working for you, this never gives you permission to check out of your finances. You need to be monitoring what is going on with your finances and how they are performing.

It's simply a fact that people steal. I hate to say it, but it's true. I would never want to see anyone taken advantage of because they have placed all their trust in a professional or assumed that the person they hired is taking care of them.

When you don't check in, you are giving up important financial control. Check your balances each month and monitor them. Question anything that seems unusual in your portfolio. Ask questions and pay attention when responses don't make sense. If you feel uneasy or suspicious, trust your gut and investigate.

Another tip is to remember that nobody will ever care about your money as much as you do. Never give your financial power away.

PROTECT YOUR WEALTH AND MITIGATE RISKS

As the business owner, you are the biggest financial asset in the business. As you generate revenue, you need to protect yourself.

Here's what you need to do that:

Emergency Funds

Emergency funds are your personal savings that help you feel financially secure. If an emergency presents itself, such as a car repair, a broken-down furnace, or some other type of urgent expense that wasn't planned for, you'll have peace of mind knowing that you have planned for it and taken care of yourself.

Insurance

You need to insure against risks. What would happen if you were no longer able to work, whether that be temporarily or permanently? Have you insured yourself against those risks?

Protecting yourself and your family against financial risks is an important part of your financial plan. You don't want to regret not having done this should you need it.

You need health insurance, critical illness insurance, and disability insurance.

Sharon Epperson is a leading CNBC senior personal finance expert who had her own health challenges. Back in 2016 she suffered a brain aneurysm, which left her out of work for over a year. She had to relearn how to walk, how to speak, and how to function as part of her recovery.

Sharon was at the height of her career and making very good money, so to have her salary disappear overnight was a financial strain for her and her family. But the good news (and Sharon often expresses gratitude for this) is that she had insurance to cover the loss of salary while she recovered.

Having critical illness insurance gets people through hard times. It's easy for you to think that you'll never need it because the chances of something like that happening to you are so low, but you will appreciate it when it's there to support you.

Wills and Life Insurance

When you have a spouse or dependents, you need to protect their financial futures as well. Wills may be an uncomfortable subject to deal with but having life insurance will help ease the financial burden for your loved ones should anything unexpected happen to you. It's a gift of legacy to leave behind.

There are endless stories of those who have passed without leaving a will and the family ends up fighting in court to gain control of the estate. However, the legal costs drain them financially and they are no further ahead in the end. Protect your loved ones by making sure to name proper beneficiaries to your life insurance and any other accounts or financial holdings that you have.

Planning for Retirement

Retirement planning is vital for business owners. Be sure to have maximized and opted in to all the financial support programs that your government offers.

Your tax accountant or financial advisor should offer advice and guidance to you on how to navigate through government programs. Then be sure to invest in additional sources.

Many investments to make to plan for retirement include investing in the stock market and/or rental properties. You can become an angel investor or move to something more creative. The opportunities are endless.

The key is that these investments will continue to appreciate and offer you additional income as they do so. Additional income can mean dividend income, interest income, and rental income.

Getting your money working for you and enjoying your retirement is ideal financial freedom.

DO NOT DEPEND ON THE SALE OF YOUR BUSINESS AS YOUR RETIREMENT PLAN

I've heard many stories where business owners bank on the value of their business when it's time to sell and retire. Markets dictate the value of your business, along with other factors that you have within your control, as discussed below in exit strategy. However, since market conditions are determined through supply and demand, you never really know how much you can sell your business for until you take it to market.

To depend on the sale of your business to fund your retirement plan 100 percent is financially irresponsible and risky. Be sure you have a diversified investment portfolio to mitigate any financial risk to your retirement plan.

Let's explore exit strategies and why you would want to think about that now, even if you think your exit is decades away.

EXIT STRATEGY

Business owners often think of their businesses as income generators, but have you thought of your business as a financial asset that can be sold when it's time to exit the business? Positioning your business to sell when you are ready to exit is not only a smart financial move, but it just makes good business sense.

Even if you aren't planning on selling your business soon, it is still wise to plan and increase your company's value earlier rather than later. Proper planning will give you extra money in your pocket at the time of sale. As the value appreciates over time, the fair market value will likely appreciate as well.

Below are the top items potential business buyers will look at when considering purchasing your business.

Strong Projected Cash Flow

Cash is queen. A buyer is looking to invest their money in a purchase that will give them a return on their investment, and the best ROI for the buyer is in cash flow. The value of projected cash flow that is already established is far more appealing to a potential buyer.

Human Capital

Particularly during the days of "The Great Resignation," where there has been a mass exodus of employees leaving their nine-to-five jobs, human capital is valuable. A well-built management team that isn't owner dependent and can function well without the owner at the helm is what investors are looking for. They want people on their team who offer value and they want to see that the business can function without your presence.

A Solid Customer Base

Having a diversified customer base with a high customer retention rate is key to adding value to a business. Customer lists of happy, satisfied, and returning customers are what buyers are looking for, and they don't want to buy a company where the customers leave with the previous owner.

Strong Supply Chain

Supply chain issues resulting in manufacturing delays and price increases are common these days, so the more robust your supply chain, the higher value your business will be. Investors value businesses that have strong relationships with suppliers to know they can depend on those suppliers.

Strong Financial Management

Having strong accounting and financial management systems in place with a strategic growth plan will position you above the competition when selling your business.

Strong Marketing Plan

Marketing your business helps get sales in the door, converting sales into cash. Having a solid marketing plan benefits the company. When you have completed the valuation and know your business is positioned well to attract a potential buyer, and market conditions dictate, you know you are ready to sell your business.

Regardless of when you are planning to exit your business, this list is something you should be implementing in your business now. The earlier you implement these moves, the earlier your business will increase equity.

Planning your exit strategy in your business will offer another layer of income that your company provides to you. When you think of your business as a financial asset that you are building to grow and appreciate over time, you can reap more financial rewards through the option of selling.

The bottom line is that I want you to be a business owner who gets wealthy from your business. This is worth repeating: being a business owner puts you in a unique position to build wealth quickly and efficiently. You have more control as a business owner over how much money you are making, and it's all generated through your business.

Getting wealthy isn't as easy as just increasing your sales. When you manage the money in your business efficiently, you are increasing the worth of the business not only as an income generator but also to sell your business in the future.

KEY TAKEAWAYS:

1. Don't be afraid of financial dreams and goals. If you have always wanted to be wealthy, know that it is possible for you.

2. Living within your means will always be the key to staying out of debt, regardless of what financial level you are at. Debt erodes wealth.

3. Know that the secret to being wealthy isn't how much money you are making but how you manage your money.

4. When you build your business as a financial asset, you are increasing your net worth.

CHAPTER 9

SET UP A MONEY ADVISORY BOARD

*"There is a gigantic difference between earning
a great deal of money and being rich."*
— MARLENE DIETRICH

They say it takes a village to raise a family; that village can keep you accountable to your financial goals as well. I have interviewed countless women who all combatted money struggles, and their secret to success was finding who—or what—kept them motivated. Money accountability partners will keep you on track. The more you surround yourself with women at your level, the more business conversations will include discussing profit margins, KPIs, and all the other fun and interesting business talk.

When I interviewed Ali Kriegsman, author of *How to Build a Goddamn Empire*, for my podcast, we talked about how people, and women, in particular, are afraid to talk about money. Many even resist calling themselves founders or entrepreneurs in the early stages of company building.

Joanna Griffiths, the CEO of Knix, was even quick to tell me when I was interviewing her for a *Forbes* article that she went eight years as the CEO of her business before she had the courage to call herself the CEO. She felt that she needed to make her title cutesy for her team and others to like her and find her approachable. She hesitated to embrace the good qualities of being a CEO for fear that she might not measure up to what being a CEO means.

These are all likely messages that we as women have heard over the years, whether it was through our formative years in school, from bullies telling us this, or from messages in mainstream media. To tune out the noise (and the haters), you need a support system.

Successful women hire and nurture a supportive team, and you need a money team as well. When you are running an empire, you need to have professionals in your corner who can advise you, but you also want to be sure you understand what they are advising you on.

Common scenarios for owner-managed businesses include having a bookkeeper or accountant on staff, a CFO to guide you, a financial advisor to help you with your financial investments, and a tax accountant to complete tax returns and offer tax optimization strategies.

There is often confusion around the roles each one plays in your business and how you work with them. Let's clear up the misconceptions now so you can engage with the right professionals who can help you on your path to wealth.

First, hire a well-trained and qualified bookkeeper. I cannot stress this step enough, as I have seen firsthand how expensive it can be to have your accounting records corrected due to shoddy work.

The bookkeeper needs to be trained and understand GAAP to do their job correctly. The bookkeeper is responsible for laying the financial foundation for your business, and you want it built solid. You run reports from the data that the bookkeeper enters, and if the data is entered incorrectly, your financial reports will be incorrect. That can be damning to your business!

Whether you outsource your bookkeeping or do it yourself, it is important to make sure your bookkeeping is accurate and up to date. I recommend a minimum of a monthly process, so at the end of the month when books are closed you can run the financial reports needed to get a complete understanding of where you stand financially in your business.

Bookkeeping errors are costly, especially when your tax accountant has to make these corrections at year-end. I have seen it so many times where a business owner pays someone to do their books, but they are not competent.

TAX ACCOUNTANTS

Often in the first few years of business when you are making less revenue, the structure is to have a bookkeeper do your books and you take your books to your accountant on an annual basis to have them complete your tax return for your business, and likely your personal taxes too. This is where a lot of business owners get confused about their relationship with their accountants.

You need to understand the terms outlined in the engagement letter. Business owners think their accountants should be offering them advice on how to improve the finances of their business. Many accountants do offer this advice, but there are also many that don't.

Professional accountants use letters of engagement to clearly outline their responsibilities, and if your accountant did not provide you with one, consider that a red flag.

Remember, you get what you pay for. If you are looking for the cheapest accountant to work with you, don't expect high-touch service. Sure, you can get a tax accountant to submit your tax return on your behalf for a nominal fee, but don't expect them to care much about your business or your tax strategies.

When searching and engaging with a tax accountant make sure they are certified (a CPA) and have experience in your industry tax laws. Also look at their other credentials and education, their work experience, their personality, and their communication skills.

BUSINESS FINANCE COACH

When you are serious about growing your business and you know that you need to get your finances in order to do so, you can choose to work with a business finance coach. They are not teaching you how to be an accountant. A good business finance coach is teaching you how to monitor your business finances at a high level, not get into the weeds of things.

When seeking a business finance coach, work with one who understands the financial landscape for businesses. Coaching is an unregulated industry, and pretty much anyone can state they are a coach, but not everyone can state they are a CPA. I suggest you look for accredited financial qualifications.

CPAs are governed by the association they belong to, which is regulated to protect the public. When you trust a CPA, you have comfort knowing they need to adhere to professional standards such as ethics and professional behavior.

Business finance coaching is what I love to do. It's satisfying for me to guide business owners through the process so that they understand what they need to know at a high level in their business to make profitable business decisions.

PART-TIME CFOS

As your business starts growing and you are earning around $500,000 in revenue and you want to jump to seven figures or more, you have to remember that what got you to $500,000 will not get you seven-plus figures in revenue. It's time to up your financial game.

A full-time CFO for a small to medium-sized business can cost you anywhere from $150,000–$250,000 per year and don't forget to add on benefits and perks. It's an expensive investment for a business to make, so you need to be sure you are ready for that commitment.

A perfect, cost-effective solution for this size of business is to hire a fractional CFO. This is a great solution because you are not losing out on the expertise of a qualified CFO but don't have to pay the full price for them. Fractional CFOs are typically kept on a monthly retainer basis and work on a reduced schedule.

It's important to hire a qualified CFO whether you are hiring part-time or full-time. You should look for an accredited professional such as a CPA and ensure they have a minimum of ten years of experience at a senior level.

Communication with the CFO is important as they are hired to be your right-hand person, the professional who offers financial guidance and advice and follows your vision.

FINANCIAL ADVISORS

Financial advisors play an important role in your investments and can guide you on personal and business investment decisions.

But beware, not all financial advisors are created equally.

Earlier, I noted this tip: Nobody will ever care about your business or money as much as you do. So never give your financial power away.

What exactly does this mean? Many of you often wonder what you are paying finance professionals for if you can't trust them completely to take care of your finances. Well, sadly, humans are human. Some humans fare OK, and some are tempted by the opportunity to do wrong.

Don't believe me? There is no shortage of stories online about people who have been taken advantage of financially.

The Institute of Internal Auditors notes in its course material that employees and advisors are more likely to steal from their business when given an opportunity to steal to do. It's when the opportunity presents itself and it becomes so easy to get away with it. This is why internal controls are so important to prevent that opportunity from happening. Close the gap and don't give people a chance to steal from you.

Part of good internal control is for you to not check out of your business and personal finances. As you grow your business and add team members into the mix, you need to prevent any fraud, embezzlement, or theft. Taking steps to implement internal controls in your business will help prevent any wrongdoing, will pay off many times, and will help you keep peace of mind.

According to the Association of Certified Fraud Examiner's 2018 report on fraud in small businesses, 29 percent of small businesses face risk due to billing, 22 percent for check payment and tampering, 21 percent for expense reimbursements, 20 percent for skimming, and 16 percent for financial statement fraud.[1]

According to the Report to the Nations 2020,[2] the top three primary control weaknesses that contribute to fraud are:

- ✔ Lack of internal controls
- ✔ The override of existing internal controls
- ✔ Lack of business owner review

When business owners step away from the financial system in their business, their absence increases the opportu-

---

1   "Report to the Nations 2018 Global Study on Occupational Fraud and Abuse," https://s3-us-west-2.amazonaws.com/acfepublic/2018-report-to-the-nations.pdf.
2   "Report to Nations: 2020 Global Study on Occupational Fraud and Abuse," https://acfepublic.s3-us-west-2.amazonaws.com/2020-Report-to-the-Nations.pdf.

nity for fraudsters. Curbing that temptation through control implementation will allow you to run your business with more confidence.

We like to trust our employees and find it hard to believe that an employee would do anything to hurt us or the business, but when we trust too much, that's when problems arise. Nobody wants to believe that a trusted employee would steal from them, but when you implement the controls to prevent that, you can avoid finding that out the hard way.

Do you really want to tempt fate?

THE COMPANY YOU KEEP

As you are building your business you need to keep company with like-minded people. They say that you are a reflection of the five people that you spend the most time with, so be sure that you choose your company wisely.

The importance of building partnerships and networking with others who can help you build and grow your business cannot be emphasized enough.

Creating a strong network of like-minded businesswomen will help keep you motivated and achieve your financial goals. There are tons of other women out there who want to achieve wealth and prosperity through their businesses, and you need to connect with them. Having these women in your social circle will elevate you, as you will them.

Surround yourself with traditional business owners who want to increase the profitability of their business and generate more personal wealth for themselves.

We need to normalize women being wealthy. There's no shame in wanting more. It does not make us greedy. I don't think it's OK to shame women for wanting more wealth and power when it's normalized by men and not out of the ordinary for a man to be financially successful.

If you are willing to work hard and make money in an honest way, where is the shame in that?

Go after big financial goals. We touched on this earlier and I will touch on it again. We need to make it completely normal for women to be wealthy and in powerful positions. The best way to create wealth for yourself is through your business, and the best way to create a successful business that will be in business for the long term is through strong money management skills.

I had a mentor tell me once that you don't need to know everything; you just need to know enough to ask the right questions. It's the same about running your business and money management in that business. The tips and knowledge in this book that I'm passing down to you will open the dialogue for more questions.

Nobody wants you to be your own accountant or CFO, but I want you to have the right amount of information to know when things are off and when it's time to question your CFO and accountants. Nobody will ever care about your business as much as you do, so never give your financial power away.

KEY TAKEAWAYS:

1. Assemble a money dream team to help support your financial goals. It takes a village to manage your business and understanding the role that each professional plays in your business is important.

2. Just because you have a team helping and advising you with your financial management does not mean you can check out. It's your responsibility to oversee and ensure your money is managed well. Ask questions, check bank statements, and read reports.

3. Building wealth is about adapting to a new lifestyle. Make friends who like to talk about wealth, growth strategies, and investment strategies. Follow finance professionals on social media, read articles, and stay current in the financial space.

CHAPTER 10

INVESTING IN THE PRESENT AND THE FUTURE

*"Your greatness is limited only
by the investments you make in yourself."*
— UNKNOWN

B y now you have learned valuable information to get you started or keep you going on investing in yourself. You will need to level up and live outside of your comfort zone most of the time.

These types of investments may involve taking courses, attending conferences, and keeping current on matters that affect your industry and business.

Being in business means that you are continually making yourself vulnerable, and that may require you to work on yourself. Consistently check in with your mindset. Invest in growth opportunities. Surround yourself with other amazing business owners who carry similar values to you.

OWN WHAT YOU'RE WORTH AND CONFIDENTLY CHARGE FOR YOUR SERVICES

As you journey through entrepreneurism, I want you to feel confident about money in all ways. Women often experience the struggle of charging what their services are worth when they venture out into business on their own. There may be a fear that if they charge too much for their services, then people won't buy from them. Or there is a case of imposter syndrome that creeps in and they question their own value and doubt that they are worth the high-ticket price. Or quite simply, they are afraid to have that money conversation with potential clients and feel if they charge lower, then they can avoid the conversation.

Do you struggle with these thoughts? You need to charge what you're worth or you will be shortchanging yourself.

You need to remember that your experience is unique to you. Own that experience confidently. You have educated yourself and you have years of experience.

The services you are offering are of value to others, and you must believe in that value. Logically you may know this, but internally you may struggle with it.

These issues that you are struggling with are also known as mind-limiting beliefs. These negative beliefs get in between you and living your best life. You can work at changing these limiting beliefs into believing in yourself and the services you offer through the following steps.

Identify Where These Thoughts Are Coming From

The thoughts and attitudes we formed about money and self-worth can go back to as early as our first childhood memories. Matt James, PhD, wrote an article titled "4 Steps to Release 'Limiting Beliefs' Learned from Childhood"[1] that explains how these beliefs can be formed at a young age. Examples of memories could be someone telling you that you are not worthy or that women will never make as much money as men. Once you identify where the beliefs originated, then move to the next step.

Consider What Triggers Them Today

In what types of situations do these memories resurface? Are there specific incidences where you find yourself questioning your worth? Do you notice a pattern? Identifying your triggers in this process is key because this is where you place your reaction to the triggers.

Explore Alternative Thoughts that Can Replace Them

When you have a list of alternative reactions that you can replace your negative thoughts with, this is where the magic happens. The more you replace your negative thoughts with positive ones, the more your attitude about money will change.

---

1   Matt James, Ph.D., "4 Steps to Release 'Limiting Beliefs' Learned from Childhood," *Psychology Today*, November 5, 2013, https://www.psychologytoday.com/ca/blog/focus-forgiveness/201311/4-steps-release-limiting-beliefs-learned-childhood.

Write down a list of positive thoughts and reactions and keep the list handy to refer to when needed.

Practice Affirmations

Affirmations are a fantastic way to start changing your views. In order to attract an abundance of money, you need to believe that you are worth it. Find a couple of affirmations that you can practice on a daily basis. Tell them to yourself in the mirror while you get ready for the day. Look at yourself and allow yourself to feel the positivity from these statements.

Let the Negative Thoughts Go

It's tiring to hang on to negative habits that no longer serve you. They drag you down and steal your energy. You need to release them and let the new, positive beliefs in.

How many women have I met over the years who are competent and excel at their services, yet have underpriced and undervalued themselves? Ladies, you need to stop this behavior now!

There is a real psychology to pricing. It's not only on the seller's end but the client's end as well. It's about perceived value. If I am looking to hire for a service that is valuable to me, I will do my research and look at the experts. Then I look at the price. But I do not base my decision solely on pricing. I also look at competence and personality.

For example, when I was hiring a coach for a project that I was working on, I had three strong professionals lined up. One charged $200/hour, one $150/hour, and one $80/hour. Ironically, my favorite out of the bunch was the one who charged $80/hour, but I did not hire her. Why? Because her lower rate was a red flag to me. If she didn't charge close to what her competitors were charging, what was wrong with her?

Her low price indicated to me that there would be less value there. I was adamant that this project was going to succeed and felt a lot of it depended on hiring the right person to help me.

Low prices attract people who do not value your services and who are just looking for the best price on something. Are these the type of clients that you want to work with?

You'll end up working harder to prove your worth to these clients because they don't value your time or experience.

I'm not suggesting you overcharge for your services. But I do want you to consider what your services are worth and the type of clients you want to be working with.

INVESTING IN A NEW PROJECT OR PRODUCT

Many entrepreneurs branch out and grow their businesses through expansions by either increasing manufacturing space, adding new products to the mix, opening new locations, or implementing many other ideas for growth.

When taking on a new project, it is important to do your due diligence and crunch the numbers to see if this new project will be profitable and worth pursuing. It's not enough (or smart) to just cross your fingers and hope for the best. This is a step most entrepreneurs don't take because you don't know what you don't know.

That's why coaching is a great way for entrepreneurs to increase their success. Be in a community of like-minded businesspeople who have your back and will help you with your blind spots.

You'd be amazed at how many projects sound really good, but when you crunch the numbers it turns out not to be such a great idea.

This also helps with new hires or new marketing campaigns. When you add these items to your business plan and start preparing for the future, seeing how long it can take to get a return on that investment will cool the idea and put it on the shelf for another time.

Timing is everything—timing not only to enter the market but also on whether it's a good idea for the business to pursue. There are many factors to consider, and qualitative factors are just as important as quantitative ones.

Raising Capital Versus Sole Ownership

When business owners need cash infusions to keep their businesses going, they turn to raising capital. There is nothing wrong with this; I just want to make sure that you understand the implications of this should you decide to go this route.

You need to be aware of what it means to get investors in your business, which likely means you are giving away part of the control. This is something that business owners don't consider when seeking cash to support their businesses.

For example, when investors are shopping around for companies to invest in, they choose companies with promise. They assess them based on various factors, and if they decide to invest in yours, they offer you the money injection that you need in exchange for a percentage ownership of your business.

If you own your business 100 percent, you have just sold part of your ownership for financing. Some investors ask for 10 percent; some are much more aggressive—it just depends on the situation. But remember, if you are giving away ownership to your business, understand that comes with influence. Many investors want to have a say in how you operate the business.

Investing Outside the Business/ Revenue Diversification

On the flip side, when you have enough wealth for yourself you can start investing in other businesses. That's part of the joy of creating wealth. There are so many ways you can create passive income for yourself. But remember, passive income is not literally passive. It requires your understanding, attention, and monitoring.

THE STAGES OF THE BUSINESS CYCLE

The early stages of business are the seed and development stage and the start-up stage.

The seed and development stage is basically when a business is an idea and no offers are put out yet. The business is busy building the internal structure of the company and working to bring products and services to market.

The start-up phase is when the product or service is ready and has gone to market. Now you're working with customer feedback to see that the product or service is what the client needs or wants. If you fail to give the client what they are willing to pay for, you are missing the mark. You need to offer a solution to a pain point the client has.

5 Stages in Business

Seed & Development -
conceptual stage, product validations. Revenue is low.

Start-up Stage -
Product iterations and continuous product development. Revenue begins to grow.

Growth & Establishment -
Generate consistent income and regularly take on new customers. Revenue is growing.

Expansion -
Business model has been proven successful. Explore other markets and look for new challenges.

Maturity & Exit -
Business has been seeing great profit and may continue to either expand or exit.

[2]

In the later stages of business, you have growth and establishment, expansion, and maturity and exit stages.

In the growth and establishment phase you are finally generating consistent income and you are taking on new customers regularly and with ease. This is where you know what you are offering is meeting the needs of your clients, and at this

---

2 "The Five Stages of Business Lifecycles," Canadian Angel Investment Foundation, https://angelfoundation.ca/five-stages-of-a-business-lifecycle/.

time you are likely focusing on growth strategies for the business. It's vital for your business to have your twelve-month operating forecast established, and you can monitor your growth against your projections.

The expansion stage is when you are ready to grow your business in terms of penetrating new markets, adding new products or services to the mix, and taking on new projects. Financial models, scenario analysis, and project valuations are used very much during this phase, as you do not want to make decisions without crunching the numbers first.

Finally, you are at the maturity and exit stage, where you are likely happy with the performance of your business, you're not really looking for additional projects to take on, and you are more concerned with investing your money and getting your money working for you. At the exit stage you also consider what you need to do to either pass down the business or sell the business to an investor.

As you build your business, I encourage clients to think about their exit strategy. You have the potential to sell your business as an asset at the end if you so desire, and we touch more on this in chapter eight.

The most important step on the path to growing your wealth is to have your money work for you. I had an amazing conversation with millionaire entrepreneur Emily Vavra, a network marketer, when I interviewed her for a *Forbes* article. We talked about wealth and managing money. Emily reached millionaire status at twenty-six and struggled a lot with spending decisions. Raised by a single mom who tightly budgeted, Emily didn't find happiness in spending a ton of money on material items. She had to create a plan to invest in the future. A five-year financial plan gives direction to your money and helps you work and attain your goals much quicker than not using one.

And even as a millionaire, Emily is not afraid to share that she still uses a budget.

A budget is a great tool regardless of where you are in your financial life because it creates a picture of how much you have coming in against how much you need going out.

But when your income increases, there is a thing called lifestyle creep, and that's where you start spending money on more things and your expenses start increasing.

A budget is a lifelong tool that you can use to help you manage your money, rich or not.

Your business is your largest asset and the quickest way to increase your wealth. When your profitability grows, your net worth grows. What do you need now to be profitable? What do you need in the future? Do you have an exit strategy for your company? Would you consider acquisition or venture capital investment?

I've worked with many business owners to whom it hasn't occurred that selling their business when they want to retire is an option. The thought is that they will just shut down the business. This is small thinking because they are only looking at the business as a revenue-generating machine when there is money in the asset as well.

When you build your business, you are building a name and creating assets for the business, a reputation, and a customer base. You may have trademarked names that are valuable as well as other assets in the business. These are valuable items that you can sell. There are many people out there who would rather buy an established business than start their own.

It's smart to look at your business as something you can sell when you are ready and to create an exit strategy for your business can bring in another income stream that you hadn't considered.

ARE YOU CONSIDERING BUSINESS EXPANSION?

Owning your business is rewarding and challenging and a rollercoaster filled with ups and downs. You put your life into building your business, and it's been going well. But have you given any thought to where you want to take this business?

If you want to grow your business and scale it, you will need to have a plan in place. Besides, as I've said before, a goal without a plan is just a wish.

Growth strategy is a plan that allows a business to expand. Growth can be achieved through investments such as adding new locations, investing in customer acquisition, or expanding a product line. A company's industry and target market influence which growth strategies it will choose.

A few points to consider when planning the growth of your business:

Look at what your competition has done—you can learn a lot from your competitors. You can see what has worked and what hasn't. Do not copy them, but you can get ideas from them.

What sets you apart from the competition—can you answer that question? Focus on your strengths and capitalize on them.

Identify your revenue streams—are you expanding through diversifying your income streams? Are you putting your business at unnecessary risk by focusing solely on one product or service? Diversifying your revenue streams in business is a smart move, as it is good to have options when one product or service isn't performing well.

Why now—is the timing right? What are market conditions like? Is there a proven demand for your product? They say timing is everything, and during expansion, that is not an exception.

Remember to stay efficient—your efficiency levels can be measured through your numbers. Be sure to maintain the level of efficiency that keeps you profitable. Be sure you know your margins and that during and after expansion you are operating within them.

Keep knowing your numbers during expansion. If you've been following me for a while, you know that I am a huge promoter of business owners knowing their numbers. This is especially true during the growth and expansion stage of a business.

The bottom line is, when you are considering growth for your business, you will have many moving parts to consider. But the most important information will be if the expansion will be profitable. There's no point in expanding your business if it does not make financial sense to do so.

Even if you don't want to sell your company now, positioning your business finances is the first step you can take in creating a financially solid company and preparing your business for future sale. Financial buyers pay attention to the numbers in your business, and they will look at the following: How leveraged is the company? How reliable is cash flow? What's the risk?

Business numbers are crucial to the sale of a business. Having your record-keeping in order is a must, as business financials are the first thing potential buyers will want information on. The more confident you are in your finances, the more attractive you will be to potential buyers. That's why it's so important to be cash confident!

KEY TAKEAWAYS:

1. Invest in the time it takes to learn this stuff. It will pay off exponentially.
2. Invest in your worth (charge what you're worth, raise your rates, etc.).
3. Invest in the market. Take fear out of the equation and learn the benefits and strategies of investing in the market.
4. Invest in your company. Ask yourself, what are the big financial decisions to make now that will pay off later?
5. Invest in the future. Create a plan for your future revenue and wealth.

CHAPTER 11

IT'S TIME TO THRIVE

"It's time to write a new story."
— UNKNOWN

Congratulations! You made it through the emotional journey to gain empowerment and build a strong financial foundation for your company's future. Now it's time to take all you have learned and continue to walk down the path toward financial freedom and to become cash confident. As the CEO *and* CFO of your life and your business, you have what it takes to realize your dreams, make a lot of money, and welcome your success.

The best part of being a business owner, in my opinion, is the lifelong learning that you've pretty much signed up for. Now I may be a bit of a nerd here, but I love the challenges that come with owning my own business. I am constantly learning and growing. Nothing in the world of business is stagnant, so survival is dependent on resilience.

It's funny because although I was a really good student up to junior high school, in my high school years I was too cool for school. Literally. I pretty much scraped by. Not my best years...

But in university and beyond my thirst for learning returned, and I'm constantly looking for new ways to do things. I prefer to learn by trying new things rather than through textbook reading, and chances are you'd likely beat me at a game of Trivial Pursuit. But I do remember random useless information like that my bestie in kindergarten's birthday was August twenty-ninth.

The point is you must keep a constant pulse on your business. You need to invest time and energy in your business if you want to grow and thrive. It's like caring for a plant. It needs special attention and to have its needs met, or it will soon dry up and die.

If 2020 taught us anything, it's that circumstances change quickly. Most of us can remember where we were when they announced the pandemic. For me it was March 13, 2020, when Prime Minister Justin Trudeau made the announcement that we were officially in a pandemic. I was on vacation; we had just landed in the Dominican Republic and basically had to fly back home two days later.

I was in my third month of business. Yep, my business was that young. But I was fortunate enough not to have left my full-time employment as an internal controls specialist yet. Being a money expert, I knew it was too risky to leave a secure job before my new venture took off. And boy, am I glad I waited. It proved to be much longer than I thought it would be for my business to generate the kind of revenue I needed to leave my steady job.

Building the business was hard work. The early days were definitely the hardest, with juggling the responsibilities of being a mom, a wife, a daughter, a friend, a head of household, and an employee. It was too much to handle, so I slowly began to delegate and use services such as Chef's Plate to deliver meals that would simplify things for me. Yet, it was so exciting!

My husband proved to be an excellent support, and I know the kids and I would have starved had he not stepped up and helped. He bought the groceries, cooked, and cleaned the house while I worked night and day, seven days a week. He believed in me and supported my dream and I'm so grateful for that.

But the main point I want to make is when you are a business owner you will be tending to your business regularly. The amount of time and attention will depend on the size of your dreams. And remember, everyone has their own dreams; you don't need to have the same dreams as other entrepreneurs.

You can run a six-figure, multiple six-figure, seven-figure business, and beyond. It's entirely your choice. The larger your business grows, the more time and attention will be required to nurture it.

Remember as you go through your journey *why* you started your business and what your big financial goals are. Know that you can be a financially confident and powerful woman and rich.

HOW WE GET IN OUR OWN WAY

I can't tell you how many times I have seen women restrict themselves from purchasing a product or service that they really do need because "it's too expensive." This is where things get sticky because my question is: is it the price or the fact that you may have some other feelings surrounding that purchase?

I have a friend who always says she can't afford something without even thinking. It's her default reaction. But what that means is that it is not a priority to her. She's not interested in making it a priority because she is too busy believing she can't afford it.

But the reality is she could afford it if she wanted it. Now, it would take some money management to get there, like stopping buying new clothes every week or giving up buying that expensive designer bag in trade for the other item. There are ways you can make things possible for yourself.

Yes, spending larger amounts of money can be scary, especially when you are not guaranteed a return. I want you to remember the return you will get when you invest in yourself. Whether it's a lipstick that makes you feel like you can change the world, or investing in skills to run your business, know that you need to believe in yourself and invest for success!

I have made smart decisions in my business, and I have made dumb ones. I have invested in the wrong courses and the wrong people and essentially lost thousands of dollars. But what I have taken away from experiences like those is that mistakes happen, and we need to forgive ourselves quickly, learn from those mistakes, and move on.

You don't want to get stuck in punishing yourself. Mistakes happen at every stage of business, but those mistakes fuel our growth as well.

I have spent decades reviewing business financial statements, and all businesses, big and small, make financial mistakes. It's part of running a business. The idea is to mitigate those mistakes and pull out of bad investments before they ruin your business.

For example, when you invest in a marketing campaign that truly feels like a winner only to find out that it is a stinker, pull the plug and move on because that's just part of business.

The worst thing you can do is self-sabotage. Forgive yourself, get out from under that mistake, and move on.

I'm not suggesting that you go all in and put yourself in debt. Just weigh the pros and cons and assess the situation carefully. Sometimes the risk will pay off, but sometimes it won't. But well-considered decisions tend to be the best and reap the most rewards.

As I've mentioned before, I once registered for a course that held great promise for my business. I was so excited to join this course because I felt that it was a perfect business model for my business. But I had only been open for business for four months, so I really knew nothing at that point and didn't get anything out of it that I could use—except the expensive lesson that it was the wrong move for me.

I chose to take the emotion out of lost money and recognize the value I gained from making that mistake. I learned what did not work for me in that business and I took some valuable information away from those experiences that have helped me better myself as an entrepreneur. Really, I kind of won in the end.

There will be more mistakes ahead for me too. The key is recognizing that it's OK to make mistakes and there is a lesson in each mistake that we make. These mistakes build and shape us and turn us into smarter businesswomen.

HOW TO THRIVE

Everything you do in your business will affect your bottom line, whether directly or indirectly. The people you hire to help you, how you manage your business, the efficiencies or inefficiencies in your business: it's all impacting your bottom line. Every decision you make for your business will have a financial impact.

It makes sense to put time and energy into making decisions that will best benefit your business. As I think of how I built my business, my parting word of advice is: network.

Don't be afraid to ask for help. I am a firm believer that business owners need a community of like-minded business owners who aren't afraid to help each other. That's why I believe so strongly in women helping women. Not only do I believe in it, but I actively do my part to help women run businesses that have value, women who take great initiative to get attention on their business.

I remember how it felt to ask women who were more advanced in their business for help and being rejected. You can't let that get you down. They may not see value in what you're doing right now, and when they do, you will have the choice again of either working with them or not.

Do not put anyone on a pedestal. Often, I see online entrepreneurs acting as though they are celebrities or that they are untouchable. I prefer to work with real people. When in business, if I am paying you for a service to help me, you should do just that. As businesspeople we cannot be an expert in every field, and if we are seeking out experts to help us, they are not above us; they are simply doing a job for us—just as we would for them if they hired us for our expertise. I have strong values and I believe that in business we should all be valued for our strengths and helped with our weaknesses. That's what makes us good businesspeople—seeking help when we need it.

If you can't think of a way you can directly help someone, think of your network and if there's a way you can connect someone with someone else who can help them. The beauty of networking is that people remember how you helped them, and it comes back to you—quite often in ways you wouldn't expect.

Don't underestimate people. Chances are when you scratch a bit under the surface, you'll see their potential.

WHY KNOWING YOUR NUMBERS WILL GIVE YOU THAT COMPETITIVE EDGE

Now that you have gone through this book, I trust that you see why knowing your numbers will help you be a better business owner, and how it benefits you.

All too often I have seen business owners intimidated by their numbers. They visit their accountants once a year to have their year-end books verified and taxes filed, but so many business owners walk away lacking the comprehension of what just happened in that meeting. It generally goes like this: here are your financial statements, this is your tax return, this is what you owe the IRS, this is what you owe accountant X, and do you have any questions…

But now you've been equipped with some financial skills that you can work on and improve. You know what you need to do to be the best, and most profitable, business owner.

Remember, numbers don't lie. These numbers offer valuable feedback on the performance of your business. They tell you when things are going well and when you need to make adjustments.

Nobody will care about your business as much as you do, and I want to help you to take full control of that business. You work hard, too hard to have others making financial decisions for you. I started my business to help hardworking business owners and managers, such as you, grow their knowledge of their numbers in a judgment-free zone.

HAVE THOSE TOUGH MONEY CONVERSATIONS

It is natural to fear what you don't know, but when you have the courage to face the fear, this is where the growth starts.

As you step into the confident business owner that you are, you will no longer fear the unknown but be excited to learn about it. If you want to push your business forward and grow your business and your wealth, you will relish learning how you can make improvements and tweaks to reach your financial goals.

As you progress in your journey as a business owner, your goals will continually change and grow, just as your business does.

This is why it's important to consistently check in with your money mindset, for that will grow and evolve as you do, and you may hit other money blocks that hold you back in your business. Set new goals, strive for more, and create the life that you truly want to live.

BUSINESS IS EVER EVOLVING; MAKE SURE YOU GROW AND EVOLVE WITH IT

Your business will lead you to a lifetime of learning. Each phase you get to in your business will offer new opportunities and challenges that you need to navigate through.

Just because you have established your business financial goals now does not mean they can't change over time. The great part about having a financial plan is that it allows you to change as you grow and learn.

Perhaps reaching eight-figure revenue levels in your business isn't important to you now, but a year from now or even ten years from now, if that changes, you are totally allowed to change your business plan.

Sometimes plans get put on hold and we can't achieve what we truly want now due to conflicting demands in life, such as caring for children and loved ones, working full-time, or going back to school—whatever your reasons, they are valid. Just remember you can always revisit a business financial plan and make adjustments.

I'm excited for you and your future! Knowing that you've picked up this book and read it tells me that you are very determined to make your business a success.

What makes a business successful? That depends on what your goals are. There is so much talk out there about getting to seven figures of revenue; the next will be eight, and I'm sure the needle will keep moving upward.

But you define your own success. And not all success is about being wealthy. Success comes from your goals and dreams, and only you can determine what success means to you.

But the key to personal success is being clear on your dreams and what really matters to you. Achieving an eight-figure revenue in business may not be important to you. Only you can decide.

Don't be afraid of big dreams; follow them. You owe it to yourself to see where they lead you.

KEY TAKEAWAYS:

1. It's your life; make it as awesome as you want. You can do this!
2. Reframe life lessons and business mistakes into positive takeaways that build on your personal experience.
3. Build financial management in your life so that you can alleviate stress and get financially confident and financially empowered.
4. It's time to soar!

ACKNOWLEDGMENTS

Writing a book is no small undertaking. It requires hours of research, writing, and editing and can often feel like a full-time job. During all this work, it's easy for other responsibilities to fall by the wayside. I'm lucky to have a husband who supports my goals and is always willing to pick up the slack. Whether taking care of the household chores or cooking dinner, he is always ready and willing to help. This allows me to focus on my writing without worrying about everything else that needs to be done. I am incredibly grateful for his support and would not be able to do it without him. Thank you, Jamie. I love you with all my heart.

As a parent, few things are more important than showing your kids how much you love them. I'm grateful for the moments when my kids show me how much they care—whether it's a spontaneous hug or a handwritten note expressing their appreciation. Those moments remind me that, despite everything, I am doing something right. I know that parenting is a tough gig, and I appreciate all the support my kids give me, especially during this book process. Matthew and Emma, you are my heart.

I want to thank my parents for their unwavering support throughout the writing of this book. Without their encouragement, I would never have had the confidence to embark on such a challenging project. I love you both so much.

Lynya Floyd, thank you for challenging me and expecting more from me and for those magical words, "Why not you?"

Jenna Kalinsky, for helping me start the process and believing my book was possible.

Kathleen Murray, for your honesty and feedback on helping me shape the book.

I am grateful for all the mentors and coaches who have helped me along the way. They have provided guidance and support, and their advice has been invaluable. I would not be where I am today without their help. I want to take this opportunity to thank them for their contributions.

Jaclyn Mellone, who has impacted my life with her kindness, generosity, and unwavering support.

And Lucinda Halpern, who has created an author's community filled with resources and support which helped shape my book.

To my literary agent, Jill Marsal, and editor, Debra Englander, Post Hill Press, for seeing the potential in this book and bringing it to life.

And for all the friends who have supported me while writing this book. It has been a long and sometimes difficult process, but your encouragement has helped me to keep going. I especially want to thank those who celebrated with me along the way, sharing my excitement as the book took shape. I couldn't have done it without you, and I thank you for being part of this journey.

ABOUT THE AUTHOR

Author photo by Lindsey Gibeau Photography

Melissa Houston is a CPA, speaker, author, and is the founder of She Means Profit, a podcast and blog that teaches successful business owners how to increase their profit margins, so they keep more money in their pocket and increase their net worth. Melissa is a contributor at large publications such as Entrepreneur, CEO World, and Forbes.